NEW MEXICO
FILMMAKING

Jeff Berg

THE
History
PRESS

Published by The History Press
Charleston, SC
www.historypress.net

Copyright © 2015 by Jeff Berg
All rights reserved

First published 2015

Manufactured in the United States

ISBN 978.1.46711.799.9

Library of Congress Control Number: 2015949274

CONTENTS

PREFACE

M y interest in films with a New Mexico connection began in earnest in 2002, although it secretly began back in 1988. I was living in Montana then and visited New Mexico as often as possible.

I had first come to New Mexico in the late '60s with my father, who had a passing interest in a printing company that was located in the village of Glorieta, New Mexico, just north of Santa Fe. I recall coming to the "Land of Enchantment" for the first time during spring break while in high school and being amazed at what I saw and learned. Being from suburban Chicago, New Mexico was even more exotic than I could imagine.

It wasn't long afterward that my father, who had decided that I *would* go to college, was able to enroll me in at the College of Artesia in southeastern New Mexico. I didn't last long in Artesia, although I loved the experience of being away from home.

A vacation trip to New Mexico (which is neither "new" or "Mexico") in 1988 changed everything. I'm not exactly sure what piqued my interest in moving to New Mexico, but going to a screening of *The Milagro Beanfield War* while in Albuquerque was certainly part of that awakening.

For the next few years, I did light research on other movies made in New Mexico and finally was able to move to Santa Fe in 1995. Financial neediness took me to northern California after just a few years, but I was able to return in 2001. When I could, I watched New Mexico movies that were easy to find and offered a glimpse of something within the state, whether it was fact or fiction.

PREFACE

When I came back to New Mexico in 2001, it was to Las Cruces, and shortly after landing there, I visited the Farm and Ranch Heritage Museum, a state-operated facility. Upon seeing the auditorium, which was not being used very much, and noting that it had a screen, comfy seats, sound and a nice VHS/DVD player, I proposed that I be allowed to use it to present movies with a New Mexico and/or farm and ranch connection. The staff readily agreed, and the series, which soon became a weekly occurrence, became one of the best draws for the museum, excluding its big events. Doing this series put my nose into the books and on to the Internet as I researched titles for the series, which was called New Mexico Connection. I was having great fun and looked forward to each Saturday afternoon and my film presentation.

In 2006, I switched venues, moving across town with a lot of folks who had become regulars of the series, landing at the Fountain Theater in Mesilla, New Mexico, which was operated by the Mesilla Valley Film Society. I was already a volunteer, and the society welcomed the program just as I welcomed the opportunity to show a larger variety of pictures, not just those that the museum was interested in.

I did the series weekly until returning to Santa Fe in July 2012, all the while writing for various publications about movies, attending and volunteering for film festivals and researching even more as I built a library of New Mexico movies, obtaining them however I could—whether they were on VHS, DVD or DVD-R.

It's been interesting. I thought there would be others who knew a lot about these movies and would allow me to pick their brains. I also wrongly assumed that there would be loads of documents that I could peruse as research material, but alas, there is hardly anything on paper except a few odds and ends.

So this book is a culmination of those years of research and, I guess, one could say development as well. I am still researching, presenting films and film clip shows around the state and finding the occasional overlooked film that brought a filmmaker to New Mexico to take advantage of the scenery, geography or tax incentive program. Or maybe it the state's famous green chile that brings them.

Do note that this is not a filmography of every movie ever shot at least in part in the state. I also do not include the thousands of short films that have been made by many talented people, and space just does not allow for tiny synopses of all of the flicks that I know exist.

I hope you enjoy this tome and take a keener interest in the finest and most creative art form on the planet.

ACKNOWLEDGEMENTS

Of course there are a few people to recognize who have helped this project come to fruition. Thank you to these wonderful people.

The late John Armijo, who was the historian for the New Mexico Film Office for many years. His support and knowledge was invaluable, as were the research papers he left me.

My late friend Lew Cady, who was the first to believe in my writing.

Author Max Evans, who not only helped start the nation's first film office but also has had more kind words for my writing than anyone on the planet.

Charles Horak, the founder and former programmer of the Plaza Classic Film Festival, and photographer Robert Yee, for their ongoing support.

Keif Henley, co-owner of Albuquerque's Guild Cinema, for his support and for hosting many of my Made in New Mexico screenings over the years.

Barb Odell, for her amazing help with photographs.

All of the folks in the audiences of any film screening that I have shared, in the past and in the future.

And of course, my wife, Sarah, for her polite toleration of all of the time I have spent on this project rather than learning how to do home repairs.

1
THE SILENT YEARS

Cinema Arrives in New Mexico

Although there were others who had similar devices that allowed for motion pictures, including William Lincoln's 1867 offering, the zoopraxiscope and Frenchman Louis Lumière's cinematographe, Thomas Edison was certainly on the cusp of something big with the Kinetoscope. Developed by Edison with help from William K.L. Dickson and Charles A. Brown, among others, the device is said to have been ready for use in 1892. Dickson also is probably responsible for the first film ever "screened" publicly (1891), a three-second experimental piece called *Dickson's Greeting*.

Neither Edison nor Lumière apparently thought much of their inventions, which would change the world, with Lumière being quoted as saying, "The cinema is an invention without a future," while Edison apparently felt that film was better suited for education rather than entertainment.

Even Lumière's first public screening of a ten-film, twenty-minute program in Paris seemed to prove him right, since only thirty-three of one hundred seats were filled. A critic at a later, more successful screening opined, "When these devices are delivered to everyone, death will cease to be absolute."

But it wasn't long before New Mexico became part of the big picture, since James White, an employee of Edison, and a crew traveling through New Mexico is credited with shooting the first piece of motion picture film in the state. They filmed on the Isleta Pueblo, south of Albuquerque, at the Isleta Indian School. The clip—which was shot in the fall of 1897 and may have been released on March 15, 1898—runs less than a minute, showing a man ushering some children out of the school and then back in again, perhaps the world's first "loop effect." Apparently, there was at least one other film made around this same time by the Edison crew while traveling through New Mexico. The troupe is said to have gone to the town of Espanola, north of Santa Fe, to make a film at the Santa Clara Pueblo. Little is known about this piece, and like many other silent films, it has apparently disappeared over time.

It wasn't until 1912 that "real" movies were shot in New Mexico, ushering in an industry that has remained viable and present for the state for over one hundred years. It was also the beginning of what could be called one of the four busiest times for movies to be shot around the state.

During the silent era—which lasted from 1908 to 1929 for New Mexico—approximately sixty movies, mostly short films, were shot in the state. The market was led by Lubin Films, Tom Mix/Selig Polyscope Company and Romaine Fielding. Lubin often shot its movies around Silver City, while Las Vegas, New Mexico, attracted Mix and Fielding, who also worked in Silver City.

Fielding—born William Grant Blandin in Kentucky in 1867—can be called the father of filmmaking in New Mexico. His film career started in New York City in 1911 with a studio called Solax. Ironically, this cutting-edge studio was owned by a woman, Alice Guy Blachè, who was also the first woman to ever direct narrative films. Fielding left Solax in 1914, joining Lubin, who was also a big name in filmmaking at the time. Lubin Southwest Company began work in El Paso, Texas, where it shot and produced six one-reel films (one reel contains one thousand feet of film). It wasn't until the company moved to Douglas, Arizona, that Fielding's name gained attention, and it was not because of his work in the movies. It was because he saved a small child from being trampled by a horse.

His spotlight in the flickers came when the company moved next to Tucson, where Fielding became director, producer and manager of the small wandering film company. He was very busy in Arizona, where he partook in over sixty films during 1912 and '13. Besides his other duties, he also wrote, acted, served as production manager and was even the special effects supervisor.

May 1913 found Fielding in Silver City, New Mexico, where he opened a studio and also supposedly looked for his brother, who was said to be an engineer for the Chino Copper Company.

His star really took off during this time, especially noted in July of that year, when the *Motion Picture Story Magazine* announced that moviegoers had selected him as "the most popular photoplayer in America." He overran such big names of the early movie business as Mary Pickford, Francis X. Bushman and cowboy star Bronco Billy. Fielding reportedly won by 500,000 votes.

Part of the reason that Fielding was probably so popular, according to the late New Mexico Film Office archivist and historian John Armijo, was because audiences could identify with his "socially conscious scenarios." Armijo wrote that Fielding's works, like that of his mentor, Alice Blanchè, "often dealt with the trappings of everyday life and the plight of ethnic peoples." Prior to Fielding's work, non-Anglo peoples were often poorly portrayed in films as "the scourge of society."

Fielding worked hard to give the characters in his movies "dignity, purpose, and humanity." He also covered issues that remain controversial even in today's films, such as addiction, sexual violence, family, interracial marriage and perhaps even an early look at post-traumatic stress disorder. Some of his works, such as *A Dash for Liberty* and *The Clod*, both of which were made in Silver City, touched on the effects that the Mexican Revolution had on the people living along the border of Mexico and Arizona. *The Clod* in particular was well received and called "flawless" by the *New York Daily Mirror*.

An opposing view of the film is offered by author A. Gabriel Meléndez in his book *Hidden Chicano Cinema: Film Dramas in the Borderlands*. Meléndez notes that the picture, which takes place during the Mexican Revolution, offering reenactments of battles, "informs filmgoers that Pedro [the main character of the film]" is "a simple-minded Mexican farmer, strong, but so dull mentally as to be a mere clod." Armijo's research revealed this praise from the *Las Vegas (NM) Optic*: "*The Clod* will long be a classic. New Fielding production sets new standard for moving pictures."

A Dash for Liberty, a story about a female detective, was a two reeler and might not have been completed. One reel of the picture is said to survive at the British Film Institute.

Fielding's shining star did not go unnoticed by others in New Mexico. Both Albuquerque and Las Vegas, New Mexico, contacted Fielding to query him about moving operations to their cities. It was 1913, and they wanted to use the upstart film industry as a method to increase economic development and tourism. In early August of that year, Fielding opted for Las Vegas and moved his studio to a rented house with a handy empty lot next door. He also leased the now-famous Plaza Hotel and, in a small fit of ego, renamed it to the Hotel Romaine. If one looks hard at one side of the hotel now, that name can still be seen painted on an outside wall. He used it to house cast and crew for his work, many of whom traveled from big cities across the country to work with the starlight that Fielding now bathed in.

It didn't take long for Fielding to get to work on making movies. He and his crew of twenty-five soon started pre-production on a film, one of the few of Fielding's works that can still be viewed, *The Rattlesnake*. A rather portentous subtitle was added: *A Psychical Species*. The film is a slightly comic/lesson-in-life piece that co-stars a you-know-what. That film, along with the next two movies that Fielding made in Las Vegas—*The Harmless One* and *The Fatal Scar*—were "hailed as masterpieces by the local and national press," as Armijo noted in his research. Gushing reviews and screenings followed these films in New York, where Fielding Night featured a double feature of *The Clod* and *The Fatal Scar*; the screening was accompanied by a full orchestra, according the *New York Dramatic Mirror*.

"The venom of jealousy has never furnished a better basis for a story than this film portrays," the *Mirror* noted when reviewing *The Rattlesnake*. Fielding's biographer, Linda Kowall Woal, heaps even more praise on the short western, noting, "*The Rattlesnake* is a western as it might have been conceived by Edgar Allan Poe."

Still, Fielding was the star of *The Rattlesnake* and helped introduce an ongoing and nose-wrinkling concept—Anglo actors and actresses appearing as Mexicans or American Indians. This remains an issue to this day in New Mexico–made movies.

By the late fall of 1913, Fielding and his company had made nine films, and pre-production work had begun on *The Golden God*, which was a drama

The rattlesnake, the star of Romaine Fielding's short silent movie of the same name. *Courtesy of the Las Vegas Film Commission.*

The cast and crew of 1913's *The Golden God*, shot in Las Vegas, New Mexico. *Courtesy of John Armijo.*

set in 1950 and a full-length feature film to boot. It had a preliminary budget of $50,000, an unheard-of amount for the times, when most films averaged $13,000 for production.

The plot of the film was described by Fielding to the *Las Vegas (NM) Optic* as being the "world-old conflict of labor and capital, culminating in a world-wide conflict, between the two."

The film included bombs, tanks, machine guns and a full choreography of war and destruction, all shot in and around Las Vegas. It even included an airplane, along with three pilots; five thousand extras; the National Guard; hundreds of horses; and two former governors of New Mexico, William Mills and Ludwig Ifield, in key roles.

The hubbub and uproar kept Las Vegas up all night every night for about two weeks until Fielding suddenly announced that he was moving his company to Galveston, Texas, for the winter. Not much is to be found about the reaction by Las Vegas and its denizens, but the film was completed in Galveston.

It had been edited from ten reels to five, and ads have been found that indicate that the film was to premiere in Philadelphia at an exhibitors

At the time of its making, the 1913 silent feature film *The Golden God* had one of the biggest casts and crews (shown) and largest budgets ($50,000) of any film. *From the archives of Moving Picture World.*

showcase in early 1914. However, the motion picture never saw the light of day since the National Board of Censorship rejected Fielding's coup de grâce because of its "inflammatory nature," "subversive nature" and "realistic battle scenes," and it was never released.

The censors may have been the only people to see the movie since all of the prints and negatives of *The Golden God* (which was the character that Fielding himself played) were destroyed, along with most of his other works, in a studio warehouse fire in June 1914.

Fielding was later fired by Lubin, but he continued to work in the craft, often as an actor and producer, working in nearly two hundred films in his career, twenty-three of them in New Mexico, before passing away in 1927.

Although most of the silent pictures are now considered lost, meaning there are no copies known to exist, several have survived the years besides Fielding's *The Rattlesnake* and Tom Mix's *The Stagecoach Driver and the Girl.* Bits and pieces of others can be found, but for the most part, the works of New Mexico's filmmaking pioneers have been lost to the ravages of time.

Mayor Ifield attempted to woo Fielding back to Las Vegas without success. The city remained determined to become a destination for filmmakers. Marketing attempts to lure Biograph and Universal Motion Pictures to the area were for naught, but in May 1915, the Selig Polyscope Company—headed by Thomas Persons, the western manager of the Los Angeles–based studio—made it known that it would be arriving in Las

Tom Mix (right), one of the most popular actors in silent films, made a number of films in Las Vegas, New Mexico, during the early years of the movies. *Courtesy of the New Mexico Film Office.*

Vegas in June to shoot some western films. With the studio came one of the biggest stars of all time, Tom Mix.

Mix, a deserter from the U.S. Army who married five times, was an instant hit and made himself and his crew available, as they often gave back to the community by performing stunts such as rope tricks and sharpshooting exhibitions for the city.

The first film finished in Las Vegas to star Mix was *Never Again*. The second, *Her Slight Mistake*, was made in forty-eight hours. The total number of films shot by Mix in Las Vegas remains a mystery. The number selected by most film historians ranges from eleven to twenty-five; Phillip St. George Cooke, New Mexico's first film historian and archivist, notes forty-six, and the *Las Vegas (NM) Optic* notes fewer than ten. The state film office offers twenty titles. Several of the films are still available for viewing, such as *Local Color at the A-1 Ranch* and *The Stagecoach Guard*.

It is interesting to note that one of the few known facts about Cooke, who began the state filmography many years later, is that he recalled being a lad of six or so and watching some of the silent films being made in Silver City.

Mix died in a tragic auto accident in Arizona in 1940. His death was almost the kind seen in bad movies. He was quite fond of his yellow Cord Phaeton and was apparently speeding down the road in it one night, some miles north of Tucson, Arizona. One of the bridges on the road was out, and Mix swerved into a gully and was struck in the back of the head by a suitcase that broke loose from the rear shelf behind him, breaking his neck and killing him instantly.

Around this time, D.W. Griffith and his film company were traveling through New Mexico on the train and stopped for a week in Albuquerque. The crew of forty, known as the Biograph Company, was on its way to New York City from Los Angeles and made two pictures in the Albuquerque area. One was *The Tourists*, a four-minute comedy directed by the great Mack Sennett and starring his then-girlfriend Mabel Normand, who was very popular during the silent era. Normand's career was cut short, as she was possibly the first Hollywood star to become a victim of scandal, fueled by her addictions.

The picture was made at the Santa Fe Railroad station and the Alvarado Hotel and Harvey House, all located in Albuquerque. The Alvarado, which is long gone, also was used in quite a few productions over the years, including several documentary clips featuring Teddy Roosevelt's visit to Albuquerque in 1916 and a few shots in the '50s for *My Friend Irma Goes West*, which featured Jerry Lewis and Dean Martin. Sennett and company also used the Barela's neighborhood, which is near the train depot and the Old Town Plaza of Albuquerque.

The making of *A Pueblo Legend*, a twelve-minute short directed by D.W. Griffith and starring silent film legend Mary Pickford, was not without its own drama. A letter that Pickford wrote to either a fan or friend offered clarity on an incident that took place during the making of *A Pueblo Legend*. She wrote:

> *Regarding the rumor that I and the Griffith Company were almost run out of town when we were shooting a picture there in 1910* [sic]. *This is true; the Indians thought we were making fun of them, which, of course, was not true. They called a town meeting including the top men of the Indian tribe, and everyone was convinced of our honesty and sincerity and so they released Griffith, who had been locked up.*

Both films, *The Tourists* and *A Pueblo Legend*, were loaned genuine Pueblo artifacts from the Fred Harvey Curio Museum and Indian Building. Pickford certainly awed the local citizenry, as she was one of the most popular actresses to ever grace the screen. During the height of her career, her salary was $2,000 a week. Both *The Tourists* and *A Pueblo Legend* are available for viewing in excellent condition from several different resources.

Several other short silent pictures were shot in New Mexico, including *The Dude*, made near Organ, New Mexico, in 1911; *Brothers*; *Fool's Gold*; and *Wages of Sin*. The same company, the Powers Motion Picture Company of New York, shot them in the Organ Mountains, near present-day Las Cruces.

Prior to these narrative short films, some documentary shorts were made at the Albuquerque Indian School, including *Fire Drill, Albuquerque Indian School*; *Carpenter Work, Albuquerque School*; and *Laguna Indian Foot Race*. These films are all considered lost.

A twenty-four-minute documentary of a boxing match between Jack Johnson and "Fireman" Jim Flynn that took place in Las Vegas has also been found in recent years. This piece, which is now restored and has narration, is from 1912 as well. It is in remarkably good shape and carries most of the fight until it is broken up by police due to Flynn's behavior.

One other short film may have been shot in northwest New Mexico by the Durango Film Company, aka the Navajo Film Company: *For Love*

A still photo from the 1898 silent film *For Love of a Navajo*, shot near Farmington, New Mexico. *Courtesy of the Farmington Museum.*

of a Navajo, made in 1922 and probably shot around Farmington, New Mexico—records remain unclear.

The *Farmington Times-Rustler* newspaper carried several breathless stories about production, noting that the crew shot eleven thousand feet of film and offering that the directors consider that "the action was good all the way thru [*sic*] the picture and the expression was excellent." The reporter goes on to share, "They consider this section ideal for making pictures, as wonderful scenery of varied types is available with a short distance from town and the dry air and brilliant sunshine make possible one of the brightest pictures ever taken."

2

THE 1930s AND 1940s

It wasn't until 1930 that another film crew appeared in New Mexico, when a film that has remained somewhat mysterious over the years was shot around Artesia, Carlsbad, Hagerman, Ruidoso and Bottomless Lake State Park, near Roswell. The working title of the film was *The Empire Builders*, but it was apparently released in 1930 in the United Kingdom as *Fool's Gold* and was also cleared for release in the United States, at least in New York, under the title *The White Renegade*. Somewhere along the line, the film was also known as *The Medicine Man*, which causes some confusion among film archivists since there was another film—which starred a very young Jack Benny—with that title released around the same time. However, that film has no connection to New Mexico.

A brief review in *Photoplay Magazine* appeared in January 1930:

> The Empire Builders—*Carlsbad Prod.*—*If you enjoyed* The Covered Wagon, *you will get a thrill out of this picture—because it is so different. Might easily be termed a burlesque on the former. However, it proves that Tom Santschi, one of the first players to make pictures in California, is an impressive, virile actor yet. Blanche Mehaffey is pretty enough for the love interest. Good entertainment for rural districts. All Talkie.*

Jed Howard, president of the Southeastern New Mexico Historical Society in Carlsbad, New Mexico, says that the first mention of the film is from October 23, 1928, and that the original film apparently was to be

A still photo from the first sound film shot in New Mexico, *White Renegade*, which is now considered a lost film. *Courtesy of Jed Howard of the Southeastern New Mexico Historical Society.*

about a fictional tribe of Native Americans "who worship the gods of the (Carlsbad) Caverns, but avoid them." There apparently is also a need for human sacrifice, which of course is slated to be the daughter of the tribal chief until her lover comes to her rescue.

Another version of the story, culled from dialogue continuity in the New York State Archives, has also been found. This version has a review noting

A quiet moment on one of the location shoots in southeastern New Mexico during the filming of *White Renegade*, possibly in 1929. *Courtesy of Jed Howard of the Southeastern New Mexico Historical Society.*

an elixir-selling doctor, gold hidden in the caverns and several plot twists related to onscreen romances.

The crew traveled around southeastern New Mexico for several months, starting in March; relocated to the Roswell area in May; and then to Carlsbad Caverns on June 24, 1929. Noted photographer Ray V. Davis, whose photos helped bring the caverns to the public eye, provided some of the financing for the film.

"The film premiered on September 29, 1929," Howard added. "And now it was called *The White Renegade*."

No copy of the film is known to still exist, although a number of stills are available through resources in Carlsbad and Artesia.

The film was made at the moment when silent films were being phased out and "talkies" were becoming the only way to release a movie. Hence, somewhere between filming and release, it was decided that the film would be made into a talking picture. It is not known whether the film was released as a silent or a talkie.

Johnny Mack Brown and Wallace Beery star as Billy the Kid and Pat Garrett, respectively, in the 1930 film *Billy the Kid. Courtesy of Western Clippings and Boyd Magers.*

Around the same time that *The White Renegade* was shooting in southeastern New Mexico, other filmmakers discovered New Mexico, with three feature films being released in 1930–31, including *Billy the Kid, Redskin* and *Way Out West.*

Billy the Kid, one of over seventy-five films (not just made in New Mexico) that have been made about William H. Bonney, was shot partially in Gallup, where part of one of the film sets still exists in storage at the historic El Morro Theater. Loosely based on fact, the film starred John Mack Brown as the Kid and Wallace Beery as his nemesis, Pat Garrett.

Brown, who went on to become a big star in B westerns (a genre of quickly made, low-budget films that were popular through the 1950s), was offered a screen test after becoming a hero of the 1926 Rose Bowl football game, helping the University of Alabama defeat Washington State.

By using New Mexico as a location, director King Vidor enabled Brown to visit with people who had actually known Billy the Kid prior to his being dispatched by Garrett in 1881. The presence of a star such as Beery playing

King Vidor, director of *Billy the Kid,* and the location crew. *Courtesy of the New Mexico/ Roswell–Area Collection of Nora Lee Davis.*

Garrett gave the film even more credibility, but it still failed at the box office—in spite of an opening statement by then governor of New Mexico Richard Dillon proclaiming the film to be "mostly true and accurate."

Some of the other films shot in New Mexico that included the Kid in one way or another include *The Left Handed Gun*, with Paul Newman; *Dirty Little Billy*, which has become the film that Kid aficionados hate the most, except perhaps for *Billy the Kid vs. Dracula* (which thankfully was *not* shot in New Mexico); *Young Guns I*; *Young Guns II*; and many documentaries.

Way Out West, another western, albeit one that included cars, was the first feature-length comedy made in New Mexico and starred William Haines, one of Hollywood's first openly gay actors (it is said that he and James Shields, his partner for fifty years, were the "happiest couple in Hollywood"), as a smooth-talking conman who cheats some cowboys out of their wages. He is caught and forced to work on the ranch to pay off the debt but also becomes a local hero in spite of his rough treatment by the cowboys. *Way Out West* (no relation to the much better known Laurel and Hardy work of the same title) was partially shot at Laguna and Acoma Pueblos in northern New Mexico. Haines, a very popular silent star, saw his career wane when

A movie poster from *Redskin*, the last silent film and the first to use color when shot in New Mexico. *Courtesy of Paramount Pictures.*

he turned to talkies and finally end when he was banned from filmmaking by Hollywood censor William Hays, for whom the Hays Code is named.

The studios that Haines worked for pressured him to forgo his gay lifestyle and to marry and father children. Haines rejected this notion, staying true to himself and his partner. Haines left filmmaking and, with Shields, opened a very successful interior design business.

The most interesting of these three early feature films is *Redskin*, the last silent film made in New Mexico. Also the first color feature made in the state, *Redskin* is highly notable due to its use of color (red), through an early Technicolor process, in its positive depiction of American Indians.

The partial use of color, while unique and artistic, happened because of budget concerns that director Victor Schertzinger used to his advantage. He made the sparse color a sort of social commentary on the way American Indians were treated. The film stars Richard Dix, an Anglo actor, but many of the extras and a few co-stars are from different tribes. The film also succeeds in being one of the first to show inter-tribal conflict, which was much more prevalent than history relates. It is an excellent film, one that has a relevant message nearly one hundred years later.

Redskin was based on a book by Elizabeth Chevalier Pickett called *Navajo*. Picket was said to be a "Navajo enthusiast" who had filmed a couple of short documentaries in the Southwest herself.

Another interesting note about *Redskin* involves Paramount Studios, which built the first road to the Acoma Pueblo in order to move equipment to that area to make the film. Prior to that, it was often a rigorous climb to the top of the mesa on which Sky City rests.

Modern-day critics often take offense at the picture, but I see it differently. It is one of the first films to ever shed a positive light on any native people, the filmmakers actually use native people to good effect in some roles and there is even a scene where Dix, as Wing Foot, refuses to honor the American flag after his hair is shorn.

Certainly, the title raises eyebrows nowadays, but in the late 1920s, injustice was a way of life to America's native peoples. That remains true today, but at least in the '20s, a small effort was made to offer a different look. It was long thought to be another lost film until a print was discovered in the 1970s, and *Redskin* is now available, restored and on DVD.

The 1930s failed to see much more in the way of moviemaking take place in New Mexico besides one film that was the first to use New Mexico as a foreign country. *The Light that Failed* (1939), based on a Rudyard Kipling book, used the terrain around Abiquiu and Espanola to its advantage, turning that area into Sudan, where the main character, an English artist, is wounded in a battle with a tribe of local warriors.

Although the film soon retreats to Britain, it remains a mystery why filming was done in this area and where the crew found extras to play the African warriors with fright wigs that attack the British camp. A great film for its time, it is still interesting to view this 1939 drama/romance. This was

Ronald Colman in a promotional picture for *The Light that Failed*, a film that has New Mexico briefly "starring" as Africa. *Courtesy of Paramount Pictures.*

the third time that Kipling's book had gone to film, with the first two pictures released in 1916 and 1923, respectively.

Air Hostess, made in 1933, also might have been made in part in Albuquerque, but it is difficult to prove this via research and watching the film. Frequent references are made to the city, and a couple of "Albuquerque Airport" signs are shown in shots, but those scenes often fade to close ups or aerial shots.

26

Left to right: Stars Jack Oakie, Jean Parker, then governor Clyde Tingley and star Fred MacMurray take a break from *The Texas Rangers*, the first of many features where New Mexico "stars" as Texas. *Rights purchased from the Albuquerque Museum of Art and History.*

It didn't take long for a New Mexico–made movie to receive the proper accolades, as 1936's *The Texas Rangers*, a western starring Fred MacMurray, received an Academy Award nomination for best sound. Gary Cooper was slated to star but was shooting a different film and was unavailable.

The film was partially shot around Gallup, Santo Domingo Pueblo and Santa Fe, in particular Diablo Canyon, which has been the setting for several other westerns over the years. An exciting and not too clichéd film, it was remade as *Streets of Laredo*, with much of the principal shooting again taking place in New Mexico, in 1949. That version starred a young William Holden and has a lot of the flavor of a film noir.

The Texas Rangers was a huge production and involved the use of some five hundred extras, including a walk-on cameo by noted San Ildefonso Pueblo potter Maria Martinez.

This was not to be the last time New Mexico "starred" as Texas, although parts of the film actually were made in Texas and then Texas governor

A poster for *The Texas Rangers*, the first film partially shot in New Mexico to win an Oscar. *Courtesy of www.doctormacro.com.*

Then governor Clyde Tingley and film director King Vidor on the set of *Billy the Kid*. Tingley actually directed a scene in the movie. *Rights purchased from the Albuquerque Museum of Art and History.*

James Allred is said to have directed the opening scene via telephone. New Mexico governor Clyde Tingley has a bit part in the motion picture as well.

Another title of note that was partially shot in New Mexico is *Grapes of Wrath* (1940), the Oscar-winning film based on John Steinbeck's Pulitzer Prize–winning novel, for which he received $70,000 for the rights to put it on film.

Directed by John Ford, the film was nominated for seven Oscars, winning two—a Best Supporting Actress for Jane Darwell and a Best Director for

Ford. The film stars Henry Fonda. There exists rumor that Tyrone Power and Spencer Tracy were considered for the part, but Fonda does a magnificent job as Tom Joad.

Otto Brower was the second unit director, and he took a crew to several states, including New Mexico, following the actual route that the Okies had taken during the Depression. All of the shots that take place in New Mexico are long shots using doubles or studio sets and not the real actors.

Another interesting note is that Brower wanted to include a shot with a large number of travelers heading west, so the business manager for the film would stop people who were actually heading west and pay them five dollars to accompany the Joads' beat-up old truck. The shots done around Gallup, Santa Rosa and Laguna Pueblo may have helped open the door for the glory days of filmmaking for the city of Gallup. Soon other filmmaking groups were also turning their eyes to New Mexico, including Republic Studios.

It was none other than Roy Rogers and one of his representatives who soon made a query to the governor's office about using the New Mexico Military Institute (NMMI) in Roswell as a location for a film. The pitch from Rogers and his associate, Ben Roscoe, was "misplaced" in the governor's office for several weeks, but the governor's office's cordial reply offered photos or "motion pictures" of NMMI or "most any place in the State of New Mexico you might desire them." The governor's office was genial, but Rogers never came to New Mexico to make a movie.

However, another production company had also been checking out NMMI, and from the tone of that letter, it appears that the other studio, probably Universal, got first dibs. The letter is typed on letterhead from "R.E. Griffith Theaters, Inc.," based in Roswell, the home of NMMI.

Another piece of correspondence has the tone of skullduggery, as a Griffith rep wrote to then governor John Miles suggesting that Rogers and company be put on hold while the state waits to see if the "other" studio will come to New Mexico. The letter read, "If the other company doesn't make a picture or doesn't make one in the next few months, then I think we should try to interest Roy Rogers, even though the production wouldn't be up to the standard we would like."

Rogers wasn't a huge star in 1940, when this correspondence was written, but it is interesting to note that even then there was a lot of behind-the-scenes cavorting going on in the world of motion pictures.

Ten years later, the Griffith Theater chain was in court with accusations of "monopolizing the first and second run exhibition of feature pictures."

Shooting a scene for an unknown western near Old Town Albuquerque, early 1940s. *Courtesy of John Armijo.*

Wallace Beery returned to New Mexico, appearing in the odd little western *The Bad Man* with Ronald Reagan and Lionel Barrymore. This was the fourth film rendition of a play written by Porter Emerson Browne and was filmed mostly in the Gallup area.

It is a romantic comedy served up with a big slice of ham, with Beery appearing as a Mexican outlaw who tries to patch up a romance. The British title of the picture was *Two-Gun Cupid*. Critics were inclined to call it *Two Gun Stupid*. The ending has Beery pulling co-star Lionel Barrymore, who is confined to a wheelchair, across the desert for a very fun joyride.

World War II didn't stop all film companies from coming to the state, with eight features shot around the state being released from 1941 to '45. Several big names made their first trek to work in the Land of Enchantment, including Randolph Scott (*Bombardier*, 1943) Lucille Ball (*Valley of the Sun*, 1942) and Howard Hughes, who shot part of a very controversial western, *The Outlaw*, with some second unit work being filmed in the Socorro area. However, it is not known if those scenes made the final cut of the original release of the film, which was edited and reedited over the years.

Due to Jane Russell's special undergarments and publicity poses like this, the release of *The Outlaw* was delayed for a few years. *Courtesy of the Wikimedia Commons.*

The Outlaw was a completely fictional (and silly) film where Billy the Kid and Doc Holliday vie for the affections of a beautiful Mexican lass, Rio McDonald, played by the sultry non-Mexican actress Jane Russell in her film debut at age twenty.

Although filming started in November 1940, the film wasn't released for the first time until 1943, when it opened in San Francisco. This was mostly due to censorship issues involving various scenes including "illicit sex between Rio and Billy," "a major criminal going unpunished" and a "trick marriage," as noted by the censors of the day. Russell's breasts seemed to be in question as well, since those same censors objected to the fact that in many scenes they were not "fully covered." An interoffice correspondence written by production code administration director Joseph Breen said this about *The Outlaw:*

> *In my more than ten years of critical examination of motion pictures, I have never seen anything quite so unacceptable as the shots of the breasts of the*

character of Rio...Throughout almost half the picture the girl's breasts, which are quite large and prominent, are shockingly emphasized.

Hughes designed special undergarments for Russell to help enhance her, ahem, assets.

It took until 1946 for the film to finally gain a full release, and even then, the manager of San Francisco's United Artists Theater was arrested and charged with exhibiting a film that was "offensive to decency." The film prints were seized as well.

The motion picture went through years of legal issues, with the end result being of course that it became hugely popular and made over $20 million at the box office, according to a 1968 issue of the *Hollywood Reporter*.

John Wayne was the star of 1942's *The Flying Tigers*, his first war picture, but he probably wasn't "in state" for the production, since only aerial shots were used, with special effects masters of the day Howard and Theodore Lydecker taking advantage of the terrain and cloud formations around and above Santa Fe.

The film is loosely based on a real group of aviators (the Flying Tigers) who volunteered to help China fight the Japanese prior to the United States' entry into the Second World War. They apparently were quite successful, as they destroyed over three hundred Japanese aircraft. The film was successful as well, since it broke all box office records at the time, making $2 million for Republic, the studio that released it. It also received three Oscar nominations.

Bombardier is another war-era film but was more of a gung-ho piece that was shot partially at Kirtland Air Force Base in Albuquerque, which was renamed Hughes Field for the film. It follows the training, duty and loves of several officers of the U.S. Army Air Force. Besides Randolph Scott, the film stars Edmond O'Brien and Anne Shirley, who, in a surprising turn for the era, plays a strong role for a woman while stuck in the middle of a romantic tug of war between the pilots. The film is sometimes viewed as being jingoistic, and that is really not arguable considering the times and circumstances.

Two of the more unusual movies filmed partially in New Mexico during the war years are 1941's *Sundown* and *The Desert Song*, released in 1943. Both involved Nazis in their curious plotting, with *Desert Song* being the first musical shot in New Mexico, mostly around Gallup.

The picture works on the concept that the Nazis are forcing Berbers, an indigenous group of North African people, to build a railroad from North Africa to Dakar. It is not such an unusual idea unless you know that

Actress Gene Tierney taking a break from her role as the mysterious Zia in *Sundown*, a film where New Mexico stands in for Africa. *Courtesy of www. doctormacro.com.*

Desert Song was originally an operetta. Led by a mysterious American, the Berbers throw off their chains and beat the Nazis into submission. It is also fun to note that one of the back lot scenes depicting a Moroccan street scene was later used in *Casablanca*, a film you may have actually heard of.

The beautiful actress Gene Tierney stars in the equally unusual *Sundown*, wherein she plays mysterious trader Zia, whose traveling caravan helps the British. Nominated for three Academy Awards, this picture was also a box office hit in 1941 and was shot mostly around Acoma Pueblo, Shiprock and Gallup. The film also offered the great African American actor Woody Strode (Woodrow in the credits for this film) his first role.

Westerns also got their due during this period, including Lucille Ball's first of two appearances in New Mexico, although her time here appears brief in *Valley of the Sun*, as most of the film appears to have been shot indoors or on sets. A comedic romance, it depicts American Indians in a poor light in spite of using extras from the Taos, Santa Clara, Jemez, San Juan and Tesuque Pueblos. This flicker was shot in part around Taos and Santa Fe. It also uses Anglo actors in the roles of noted Apache war chiefs Geronimo and Cochise and lost over $150,000 at the box office.

A short film that deserves notice is the propaganda/recruitment film *Son of the Conquistadors*, which was shot in northern New Mexico in 1944 and was used to try and enlist Hispanics into the armed forces.

Sudan, certainly one of the more atypical pictures shot in New Mexico, starred Jon Hall and Maria Montez in a comedy/drama that was made around Gallup. Montez and Hall had made five previous movies together, and this was their final pairing. Andy Devine, a noted character actor, appears as Hall's sidekick in a costume that must be seen to be believed.

John Wayne looking mystified about why he took his role in *Without Reservations*, partially shot in far northern New Mexico. *Courtesy of the Wikimedia Commons.*

Without Reservations made a brief stop in New Mexico in 1946. Momentarily featuring Raton, located in far northern New Mexico near the Colorado border, the film is based on a novel called *Thanks God, I'll Take It from Here*. It is a romantic comedy that follows a ditzy female author whose book is about to be made into a movie. Her misadventures with two returning World War II vets have them traveling to California.

The film features John Wayne—although he was probably not ever in New Mexico, a fact that is verified by a letter from his office to the state film office (he later did come to New Mexico to make the superb western *The Cowboys*)—Claudette Colbert and Don DeFore. This is a fun and frivolous flick and clearly shows some brief second unit shots of downtown Raton.

The year 1947 was a banner year for movies made in New Mexico. Five pictures were shot at least in part in the state, including the recently restored film noir piece *Ride the Pink Horse*; *Pursued*, an "adult" western; *The Sea of Grass*, starring Spencer Tracy and Katharine Hepburn; and a rather scary docu-drama, the first one centered on the atomic bomb, *The Beginning or the End*.

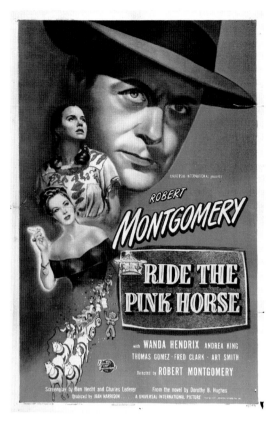

Ride the Pink Horse, New Mexico's first film noir, was shot partially in Santa Fe. Co-star Thomas Gomez became the first Hispanic actor to win an Oscar for his work in this picture. *Courtesy of the Wikimedia Commons.*

Clark Gable also made his only stop in New Mexico when he came to Albuquerque to shoot a few scenes for *The Hucksters.* The scenes are at the old Santa Fe train depot in Albuquerque. The film stars Deborah Kerr and Sydney Greenstreet and is based on a *Saturday Evening Post* article that exposed how an advertising agency was controlling much of the entertainment market at the time. The film set a record for the time, opening in one thousand theaters in July 1947.

Ride the Pink Horse and the western *Pursued* introduced the state to the genre of film noir.

Ride the Pink Horse, although set in a fictional New Mexico town called San Pablo, uses scenes of downtown Santa Fe as a backdrop along with the city's famous Zozobra festival. The press notes for the film offer that San Pablo is a blend of the "Hispanic areas of Albuquerque, Santa Fe and Taos, New Mexico." Director Robert Montgomery also stars as a veteran who comes to town to settle a score with a vacationing mobster and is assisted by Thomas Gomez, who operates a carousel with a pink horse. Wanda Hendrix plays a young Mexican woman, Pila, who takes a shine to Montgomery's character, Lucky Gagin, for reasons that aren't totally clear.

The town of Taos was supposedly paid $2,000 for the use and shipment to California of its infamous Tio Vivo Flying Jenny carousel, which was built in 1882 and has been in use by the Taos Lions Club for festivals since 1939.

The film is based on a book by Dorothy Hughes and is only flawed by having an Anglo (Hendrix) play the part of a Latina. Everything else works, even if the by now famous Breen Office had some concerns about the amount of drinking in the film. Gomez was nominated for a Best Supporting Actor Academy Award, and the film has recently started to receive long-past-due attention after the release of a DVD that is enhanced with numerous extra treats.

Pursued brought Robert Mitchum to New Mexico for the first time, along with director Raoul Walsh, who made several westerns in the state.

This one was shot mostly in the Gallup area again, using the area's western-looking landscape as a backdrop for this dark and adult film. Mitchum's character, Jeb, was orphaned at a young age. He has troubling memories and has now returned to find the man who killed his father. Mitchum's role was intended for Fred MacMurray, who apparently turned it down.

Walsh, who directed over one hundred films during his lengthy career, took a liking to New Mexico, as he returned in 1949 to shoot *Colorado Territory* and in the early '60s to film another western, *A Distant Trumpet*, which was his final film as a director.

He also gave John Wayne's career a boost by casting him in the lead of the non–New Mexico 1930 release *The Big Trail*, and he also met and rode with famed Mexican general Pancho Villa, making a documentary about him that is said to have included the execution of some prisoners, something that Villa made Walsh film.

His films were seldom light, and actor Jack Pickford once taunted Walsh by telling him, "Your idea of light comedy is to burn down a whorehouse." Walsh approved of the quip and repeated it often.

The Sea of Grass successfully paired Spencer Tracy and Katharine Hepburn in a rather sprawling western that, oddly, takes place mostly indoors. This is quite possibly because of Tracy's dislike of filming on location, so one will assume that he never came to New Mexico for the few brief outdoor shots in this film. Insert shots of the Plains of San Agustin, near Socorro in central New Mexico, depict Tracy's sea of grass as the land he owns. There are also other brief scenes near Gallup, and a "replica of a New Mexico town" of the 1880s was built on the back lot of MGM studios. It's a rather dull affair, all in all, although it was one of the highest grossing films of the year, bringing in more than $3 million.

Most of the film was done on a sound stage, using a rear projection screen. Director Elia Kazan was not pleased with this and in an interview some years later said, "I should have quit as soon as I heard that. I'll never be a studio director."

The other film shot partially in New Mexico in 1947, *The Beginning or the End*, purportedly told the true story of the development of the atomic bomb in New Mexico. The film was the first to touch on the subject and was originally questioning the use of atomic energy. But by the time the film was made, with approval by then president Harry Truman, the picture did quite a turnaround, becoming a proponent of the idea rather than issuing caution. It is part documentary, with portions of the film being shot in the Los Alamos area, and part drama. It even received an Oscar nomination for Best Documentary. It would have been nice to see how the picture would have fared had it been allowed to follow its original anti-nuke storyline.

The end of the decade saw six more westerns filmed in New Mexico, including *Four Faces West* (1948); *El Paso*; *Streets of Laredo*; *Colorado Territory*, which was Raoul Walsh's remake of the great Humphrey Bogart film *High Sierra*; *Ambush*; and Gene Autry's only venture across the state line, *Sons of New Mexico*. All of these films came out in 1949.

Autry crossing the state line was supposedly only for the film's theater premiere. The loose editing of the film clearly shows that Gene is not where he says he is, sorry to say, and neither is Champion, the Wonder Horse. It's that infernal rear projection (actors on a soundstage with a superimposed background) again, meaning that he probably did his work in California.

This film, said to be one of Autry's best, has more production and continuity errors than almost any film I have ever seen, but it is still a cut above a lot of his work. Autry does sing and pursue bad guys, all in the Roswell area, making this the first film shot in eastern New Mexico in almost thirty years. It also uses the New Mexico Military Institute as a setting and offers Autry's first pairing with actress Gail Davis, who went on to appear in many more of Autry's works. She became a star via the *Annie Oakley* TV show. Clayton Moore, the original Lone Ranger, makes an appearance as well.

El Paso, a small film with a million-dollar budget, was another picture that used the Gallup area for part of its location shoot and was also the first of a spate of New Mexico–made westerns that have a Civil War theme. Although New Mexico did see some Civil War activity early in the war when a column of Confederate troops claimed New Mexico Territory—making Mesilla, a town in the southern part of the state, the capital and also taking Tucson, Arizona—there was not nearly the activity that was depicted on the silver screen. Two battles later, one near Socorro and the other north of Santa Fe, the Confederate invaders fled for friendlier confines.

Singing cowboy star Gene Autry made one hundred films but only one in New Mexico. It is thought that all of his scenes were shot in California and edited into *Sons of New Mexico*. *Courtesy of the New Mexico Film Office.*

El Paso stars John Payne, a reliable leading man for many years, and Gabby Harnett, along for the ride to offer comic relief. The story takes ex-Confederate Payne to El Paso as a lawyer who turns into a vigilante after discovering that the town is under the thumb of one man, Bert Donner (Sterling Hayden). Gail Russell, a fine actress in her own right, adds some balance and charm to this standard western.

Four Faces West, on the other hand, is a western that everyone involved can be proud of. It stars Joel McCrea as Ross McEwan, a down-on-his-luck cowboy who robs a bank, leaving an IOU for $2,000 signed "Jefferson Davis." Pat Garrett, the new sheriff of Santa Maria, is soon in hot pursuit.

There are a number of things that make this film several steps above the standard western picture of the era:

- There are no gunshots, and no one dies by any other means.
- It is the first New Mexico–made film that I have discovered that offers a strong lead character who is supposedly of Spanish or Mexican descent. Alas, the actor that plays Monte Marquez is actually the Malta-born Joseph Calleia, who had a strong career but often played characters of Spanish descent.
- It is based on a novelette by Eugene Manlove Rhodes, an author who lived in southern New Mexico off and on for many years, trying his hand and succeeding at various jobs before turning to writing as a full-time vocation. He once owned a six-thousand-acre ranch near the town of Alamogordo and is buried in that area.
- *Four Faces West* was one of the first films to use much of New Mexico as its location, including El Morro, El Morro (Inscription Rock), White Sands, Alamogordo, the village of San Rafael in northwest New Mexico and, of course, Gallup.
- It features a "real" cowboy, which occurs when McCrea is trying to elude the posse and switches his saddle from his horse to a longhorn steer and rides off.

Ambush is one of the best of the other three late '40s films. It stars Robert Taylor as a reluctant scout for the cavalry that accompanies a troop in search of a kidnapped woman. It is notable for three things, besides the fact that some of the location shooting was done near Gallup, New Mexico, including a few raised eyebrows from the depiction of Arlene Dahl's character, which included hints of adultery, spousal abuse and some gently revealing costumes.

The screenplay was written by a woman, Marguerite Roberts, which probably is one of the reasons for Dahl's character being in the situation that she was. Roberts's other screen credits include *The Sea of Grass, Red Sky at Morning* and *Shoot Out*, all of which were made at least in part in New Mexico. She was also the screenwriter for the original version of *True Grit*.

This was also the last film made by Sam Wood, a noted director, who died shortly thereafter from a heart attack. Wood founded the Motion Picture Alliance in 1944, which was a group of Hollywood types that tried to find out who in the motion picture industry were communists or sympathizers. It is said that he was so driven by this mission that it, combined with working at high elevations during the shooting of *Ambush*, led to his demise. One wonders how he would have reacted knowing that Roberts was among those blacklisted in 1952 for refusing to name names in testimony to the House Un-American Activities Committee.

Colorado Territory also stars McCrea, and many critics think it is better than Walsh's Humphrey Bogart vehicle, *High Sierra*, which he directed in 1941, although it was the first American movie to be banned in West Germany, where censors called it "an example of gangster films which glorify anti-social elements." And once again, we return to the Wild West region around Gallup for partial shooting of the film.

William Holden was the star of *Streets of Laredo*, a remake of *The Texas Rangers*, which was covered earlier in this book. Holden and his two cohorts turn from bad guys to good guys when they join the Rangers, galloping across the scenic wonder of Gallup, New Mexico. It also makes great use of shadows throughout.

3

EUREKA! NEW MEXICO IS DISCOVERED

The 1950s

The end of the '40s found an open door for New Mexico–made movies, especially in the 1950s, when over thirty productions were shot within state boundaries and television discovered the state as well. In all of the years of research I have done on this subject, I have yet to find any definitive reasons as to why so many filmmakers came to New Mexico prior to the days of film incentives. There have been two pre-incentive periods where that has happened, which will be discussed later.

Many of the films shot in New Mexico in the 1950s were westerns. In 1950, there were six productions that included several big names of the times, such as Deborah Kerr, Errol Flynn, Bob Hope, Jerry Lewis, Dean Martin and Stewart Granger.

King Solomon's Mines, yet another remake of the story, starred Kerr and Granger. Although the tagline read, "Filmed entirely in the wilds of Africa," that was strictly studio bluster since portions of the film were shot in Carlsbad Caverns National Park, around the town of Carlsbad and in White Sands National Monument. And let's hope that they didn't move Death Valley, California, to Africa, since some location shots are used from that beautiful place as well.

The film was nominated for three Oscars, including Best Picture, which was the only award it failed to win. The movie won the awards for Best Film Editing and Best Cinematography. It also won a Golden Globe for Robert Surtees's cinematography. It is a beautifully shot picture and is certainly the best of the six versions of the same book that have been put onto film.

A one-sheet poster for *New Mexico*, released in 1951. *Courtesy of the New Mexico Film Office.*

Bob Hope first set foot in New Mexico to make a film when he shot the comedy *Fancy Pants* with Lucille Ball as a co-star. Hope plays a hapless actor masquerading as a butler who comes west with a wealthy English family as the lady of the house tries to instill some refinement into her husband and daughter (Ball). Hijinx ensue.

Fancy Pants was partially shot around Santa Fe and Lamy, New Mexico. At one point, production was halted after Hope fell off a mechanical horse and experienced a mild concussion.

The first feature film of the decade shot in Albuquerque was the B western *Short Grass*, which starred Rod Cameron, who was noted for his frequent roles in that genre. A standard western, having small ranchers being bullied by big ranchers, *Short Grass* was the only film—of the nearly 125 films and television shows that he worked on—that Cameron made in New Mexico.

Martin and Lewis came to New Mexico, albeit briefly, to shoot the sequel to the very successful *My Friend Irma*, with this film being called *My Friend Irma Goes West*. The picture has an embarrassing scene, filmed at the Albuquerque train station, where Lewis ends up dressed as an American Indian trying to sell trinkets. It might be one of the most racist scenes ever put on film.

Martin and Lewis returned in 1956 to shoot *Hollywood or Bust* as they breeze through downtown Santa Fe and points west on a road trip in a shiny new red convertible. Lewis rides in the trunk of the car with a Great Dane, while Martin drives with a beautiful woman, played by Diana Lynn, sitting next to him. The picture was produced by Hal Wallis, whose wife, actress Martha Hyer, moved to Santa Fe in 1986. This was Martin and Lewis's last picture together, and tensions were said to be high.

Rocky Mountain (1950), a well-photographed and action-filled western, featured the fading star of Errol Flynn. Screenwriter Winston Miller later shared that the director of the film, William Keighley, and his wife knew all about Flynn's flirty behavior around women and tried to protect co-star Patrice Wymore, who was appearing in her first film, by having the two stay at opposite ends of the hotel while on location, with Keighley and his spouse in the middle of the hotel.

It was nothing more than a noble effort to protect Wymore, since Flynn must have gone around back for meetings with her, and she soon became his fourth wife after he dumped his then girlfriend.

That hotel was probably the famed El Rancho, located in Gallup, New Mexico, which hosted dozens of stars during the heyday of moviemaking in Gallup in the 1950s. The hotel was formally opened on December 17,

1937, and was owned by R.E. "Griff" Griffith, brother of famed director D.W. Griffith.

The brothers encouraged filmmakers to use the beautiful landscapes around Gallup to film their movies, often westerns, while also encouraging use of the El Rancho as a place for the cast and crew to stay during filming. The El Rancho was a beautifully appointed place with a western motif and became host to dozens of stars besides (possibly) Flynn and Wymore. Some of the many who slept in the hotel include Burt Lancaster, Ida Lupino, Jack Benny, John Wayne, Jean Harlow, Kirk Douglas, Rosalind Russell and even W.C. Fields.

The El Rancho's star has faded since it was the headquarters for about fifteen films from the late '30s until about 1964 since it has been a long time since a major film has been shot in the area. The El Rancho still hosts nostalgic travelers, many of whom view it as an iconic symbol of Route 66.

One of the best films ever shot in New Mexico was made in the Gallup area in 1951. *Ace in the Hole* (aka *The Big Carnival*) stars Kirk Douglas and Jan Sterling.

Douglas plays a once famous newspaper reporter who has fallen on hard times and has been booted off of the staff of almost every major daily paper in the country. His car breaks down in Albuquerque, and the fast-talking Douglas soon wrangles his way onto the staff of the *Albuquerque Sun Bulletin*

Kirk Douglas from his superb performance in *Ace in the Hole*, offering "lunch" to co-star Jan Sterling. *Courtesy of www.thedissolve.com.*

and is assigned to dull local stories in the then-small city. One day, while on assignment with a young photographer, Charles Tatum (Douglas) stops at a rural trading post that turns into a potential gold mine for the cynical and egotistical Tatum. It seems that a local man has been trapped in a mine cave-in, and soon Tatum has turned the poor trapped man's story into pure headline fodder. With that come crowds of people to the trading post, ensuring that the trapped man's wife will be able to make enough money to escape her own rural entrapment.

The carloads of lookers arrive at the post and pay to see the "rescue" operation. A carnival is even set up, which more or less led to renaming the film *The Big Carnival*. It was a box office and critical flop. It fared much better in Europe, receiving high praise from British critics and winning the International Prize at the 1951 Venice (Italy) Film Festival.

"Too cynical," critics and audiences cried, but one might think otherwise, since it is directed by Billy Wilder, whose résumé at the time included mostly musical comedies, not edgy and porous film noir. Wilder was never informed of the title change, but the film did not do any better than it did as *Ace in the Hole*. The original title was *Human Interest Story*, but that never saw the light of day.

Besides its box office troubles, the film was beset with lawsuits due to the fact that it was based on a 1925 incident in Kentucky where Floyd Collins, searching for a new entrance to what is now Mammoth Cave National Park, became trapped when a rock fell on his foot. A young reporter was able to squeeze into the area near Collins, talking to him and bringing him food. However, during the rescue attempt via a vertical shaft, there was another collapse, and Collins died before the rescue could take place. The same thing happens in *Ace in the Hole*. The Kentucky reporter, William Miller, won a Pulitzer Prize for his work on the story, which also created a carnival-like atmosphere around the scene of the tragedy.

Ace in the Hole cost $1.8 million to make, with $30,000 of that being used to create the cliff dwelling set, which, at the time, was the biggest set ever built for a picture that was not a war movie. The cave dwellings behind the trading post were built especially for that movie and were located at Christensen's Cliff Dwelling Trading Post, at Lookout Point, New Mexico, west of Gallup.

It was a gigantic set, soaring 237 feet into the air and covering an area 1,200 by 1,600 feet. Over one thousand locals were hired as extras, including a large group of Navajo and Zuni Indians. They were paid seventy-five cents an hour for a ten-hour work day. Those with cars received three dollars more

Kirk Douglas addressing the masses in *Ace in the Hole*. *Courtesy of www.dissolve.com.*

if they drove to the set. Wilder predicted correctly that people would show up at the film shoot anyway, so extras were many and easy to find. The cliff dwelling was left intact as a tourist attraction, but both it and the trading post are now gone.

One of the film world's biggest directors also got a start in New Mexico when he came in 1951 to shoot the short film *The Flying Padre*. Stanley Kubrick (*A Clockwork Orange, 2001: A Space Odyssey*) came to eastern New Mexico to film the ten-minute documentary after receiving an advance from the RKO Studio. The little film follows Father Fred Stadtmuller, who used a Piper Cub airplane to cover his parish, which measured four hundred square miles. Kubrick, in a late '60s interview, noted that he thought the film was "silly." Personally, I've seen worse. Much worse.

Other big-name stars made their way to New Mexico in the early '50s as well, including Gregory Peck and Lon Chaney Jr., who starred in a western based on *Only the Valiant* by Charles Marquis Warren.

Again shooting around Gallup, the film was to originally feature Jimmy Cagney, who did come to New Mexico a bit later to shoot *Run for Cover*, which was partially shot around the Aztec ruins near Farmington in northeast New Mexico. Gary Cooper was also approached for the lead, but it was Peck who landed the role, later saying it was the least favorite of all of his movies.

From 1952 through 1956, there was a slight swing away from westerns, with only five of the thirteen films shot here being of that genre. Except for *Hollywood or Bust*, the stars stayed away as well, with only smaller films and a couple of documentaries being made.

Perhaps the best-known actor who came to the state during this time was Jimmy Stewart, who played in *The Man from Laramie*, which has New Mexico starring as Wyoming.

Among the non-westerns were two film noir pieces, *Make Haste to Live* and *The Atomic City*. *Make Haste to Live*, based on a novel by Mildred and Gordon Gordon (yes, that's correct!), was also known as *The Outcast* and *Woman in the Fog*. Partially shot in Taos and near Santa Fe, it was poorly received in spite of a strong cast headed up by Dorothy McGuire, who ran the town newspaper. McGuire's part is a strong female lead, something that there wasn't much of in the 1950s.

New Mexico's history with the atomic world again came into view with the release of *The Atomic City* in 1952. More of a spy story with a bit of film noir thrown in, this movie, which stars Gene Barry, was the first to be able to use footage from what was then the main gate of the Los Alamos Scientific Laboratory, along with other work being done in Santa Fe. A few scenes may have been shot in Los Alamos proper, but that is still a subject of debate.

Another noir-type film is *Ring of Fear*, which might actually be more of a chase movie than a true noir. But the unusual casting is what might catch one's eye—the film stars Mickey Spillane, the author, as Mickey Spillane. Not to be outdone, Clyde Beatty, a household name when this movie was made, also stars. Beatty, no relation to Warren Beatty, was the operator of the Clyde Beatty Circus, which was one of the largest in the country back then. Beatty himself was quite popular during this time, hosting a radio show from 1950 to '51. He also made several television appearances and before this film appeared in several others, including the Abbott and Costello comedy *Africa Screams*.

In this case, it is not hard to figure out why a portion of the movie was shot in Deming, New Mexico, in the southwest corner of the state. Deming was the winter home for the circus and offered the opportunity to list the Wallenda High Wire Act and the Beattyettes Iron Jaw Display as co-stars. Originally, the film was to be shot in 3-D, but it was probably budget restrictions that laid that idea to rest.

A newspaper ad for *Ring of Fear*, a 1954 release shot partially in Deming, New Mexico. *From the* Grand Island (NE) Daily Independent.

It was also during the '50s that one of New Mexico's most revered and iconic pictures was made, *Salt of the Earth*. Shooting in the Silver City area, the film was based on the true story of a miners' strike but went far beyond that, embracing the fight for equal rights for Mexican Americans who were being assigned substandard housing by the mining companies, not to mention having separate restrooms, pay windows and other indignities of racial bias, including lower pay. The movie also included a subplot about the mistreatment of women.

The film was directed by Herbert Biberman, who started the Independent Productions Corporation with Simon Lazarus and Paul Jarrico. Using mostly non-professional actors, including many of the actual striking miners and their families, filming ran into numerous complications, including having the crew and cast being asked to leave the area by local citizens.

Biberman's company was formed to employ blacklisted filmmakers who had been figuratively tarred and feathered during the McCarthy witch hunt days. Some unions, including some union projectionists, refused to work with the filmmakers once the film was ready for release. Accounts vary about where it was first shown—possibly in an independent theater in Yorkville, New York, or at the Sky-Vue Drive In in Silver City, where it supposedly ran for three weeks. A California congressman, Republican Donald Jackson, was quoted as saying that *Salt of the Earth* was "deliberately designed to inflame racial hatreds" and was "a new weapon for Russia."

The film languished for many years and never had a real release in spite of the fact that it won awards at the Prague (Czechoslovakia) Film Festival. Actress Rosaura Revueltas, a noted Mexican actress of the times, later found that her career in film had pretty much come to an end. She was blacklisted by the Mexican film industry but had a somewhat successful career in live theater. The movie is now seen as a historical masterpiece and fills theaters whenever it is shown in New Mexico.

It wasn't until 1958 that television found New Mexico, with the production of the *Nine Lives of Elfego Baca*. The show had ten episodes on Disney's Wonderful World of Color. Robert Loggia, an Italian American, played the part of Baca, which was unfortunately commonplace back then. The show was based on Baca's true story, which took place in what is now Reserve, New Mexico.

The true story of Baca is an amazing one to say the least. A deputy sheriff in what was then Frisco, New Mexico, Baca arrested a cowboy who had shot him, raising the ire of numerous other Anglo cowpunchers, who trapped him in a flimsy shack, firing over four hundred bullets into it but never hitting Baca. He survived with a little help from his friends and went on to become a successful lawyer, private detective and, later, a politician.

Television returned in 1960 when the hit series *Route 66* filmed a few episodes in the state, three in northern New Mexico and one at Carlsbad Caverns. Oddly, unless one is a purist, not a single episode of the show, which touched on many social issues of the time, was ever made on or near the infamous highway, unless you count the Santa Fe episode, which was done long after 66 was rerouted away from Santa Fe.

The decade closed with a few other productions, including *The Left Handed Gun*, with a young Paul Newman starring as Billy the Kid, which was partially shot around Santa Fe. The film was directed by Arthur Penn, who became famous about ten years later when he directed *Bonnie and Clyde*.

The debate about which hand William Bonney (Bonney being Billy the Kid's supposed real name) used has come into focus over the years. Back then, the only known photo of Billy shows him with his holster on his left hip and a rifle in his left hand, which would naturally lead one to believe that he was left handed. However, for many years, no one remembered that the type of photo he appeared in reversed the image, thus making it appear that his right hand was his left. It is now pretty certain that the Kid was right handed after all. It is also believed that he spoke Spanish, was a ladies' man and loved to dance.

The '50s ended with a big film and a little film. The big one, *Journey to the Center of the World*, was shot partially at Carlsbad Caverns and starred Arlene Dahl, James Mason and a young Pat Boone, who had to be talked into making the picture by his agent but

A deadly serious Paul Newman, the star of *The Left Handed Gun*, an esoteric story of Billy the Kid based on a play written by Gore Vidal. *Courtesy of www. fiftieswesterns.wordpress.com.*

later admitted that he was glad he did since it was the role that most people remember him for. The residual checks were nice, too!

Journey to the Center of the World was nominated for three Oscars, had a budget estimated at $3.4 million and has since been remade several times.

But the other film, a suspenseful little crime drama, hasn't been seen by a lot of people over the years. *Date with Death*, with a budget of a mere $60,000, might be one of New Mexico's best unknown movies. It was shot mostly in the Roswell area and tells the story of a drifter who assumes the identity of a dead policeman and helps clean up a crime-ridden desert town. The film stars Gerald Mohr, who had a busy but short career, making nearly fifty movies in twenty-five years.

And again, why would a production company come to Roswell, New Mexico, to make this film? Certainly there is nothing wrong with Roswell, but how did the location manager ever find "just the right spot" to shoot this well-written drama? And why would they add a process known as "Psychorama," a filmmaking method developed by psychologist Dr. Robert E. Corrigan? In one of the reviews found for the picture, it is noted that "the process inserted subliminal messages within the film, words or images that were flashed onto the screen to alert or otherwise affect the audience." The messages were "too fast for the eyes to readily see but perceivable by the subconscious mind." Only poor-quality copies of the film exist at this time, so we may never know what those messages were.

4

NEW MEXICO GROOVES IN THE 1960s

B ig things were on the horizon for New Mexico movies when David Cargo was elected governor in 1967. He, along with some other visionary types, formed what would later become the New Mexico Film Office. Prior to that, the film industry in New Mexico fizzled for most of the decade.

Between 1960 and 1967, only ten film crews came to New Mexico, and most of those were for small productions. The first film shot in the state in the '60s was *Wild Youth*, which was most likely shot in and around Tucumcari. The film starred Carol Ohmart, one of many blond actresses being prepped to steal some of Marilyn Monroe's limelight. A year after Paramount Studios spent $2 million trying to push her star to the top, her contract was dropped. The rest of Ohmart's life sounds like a sad movie fable, going from the top to the bottom and being put upon for years by her unbalanced mother. The film was later retitled *Naked Youth*, but since no such people appear in the film, it quickly disappeared from theaters.

In 1962, another of New Mexico's all-time top ten films was shot in the Albuquerque area and in the Sandia Mountains. *Lonely Are the Brave*, based on the novel *The Last Cowboy* by Edward Abbey, brought Kirk Douglas back to the state to film what he claims to be his personal favorite film of all that he has made. During an interview on a DVD extra, Douglas relates:

> *I love the theme that if you try to be an individual, society will crush you. I play a modern-day cowboy still living by the code of the Old West.*

Then versus now: Kirk Douglas and his horse Whiskey proving that they don't want to adjust to the times in *Lonely Are the Brave*. *Courtesy of www.nj.com.*

Dalton [Trumbo] *wrote a perfect screenplay—one draft, no revisions. My character gets into a bar fight with a vicious one-armed man. He was actually Burt Lancaster's stand-in, who had lost his arm in the war.* [Also, the same actor who starred as the one-armed man in the television series *The Fugitive*.]

It was a tough shoot in and around Albuquerque—high altitude, snow, fog and freezing rain in May! I didn't get along with the director very well; plus, he had no regard for safety. When we were shooting on a narrow ledge with a steep drop, he asked me to walk around my horse on the outside. I wanted to be on the inside against the wall, because the horse instinctively would protect itself. Even after I explained, he argued with me, but I had seen too many unnecessary accidents to agree. The best relationship I had on this film was with my horse, Whiskey. Of course, the horse couldn't talk back!

The film also stars Walter Matthau and is a modern-day western that has Douglas, who did his own stunts, on the run from the law after escaping from jail. He has been tossed in jail while trying to help a friend, but he clearly is unable to accept modern times, preferring to live under the stars with his horse.

It is a tense and believable film, directed by David Miller, whose career in directing went from 1939 to 1981. He also directed another movie that used a bit of New Mexico, the previously mentioned *The Flying Tigers*.

Some other television works kept cameras rolling in New Mexico through the rest of the '60s, including the successful *Empire*, which premiered in 1962, and *The Devil's Mistress*, the first film shot in the Las Cruces area since the days of silent films. Written and directed by Orville Wanzer, then an instructor at New Mexico State University, *The Devil's Mistress* might also be the first vampire western. Wanzer convinced a lot of people to work for free, and the film actually got a release in New York, according to Wanzer, who came out for a special screening in Las Cruces in 2011.

However, things started to change drastically in 1968. Clint Eastwood came to New Mexico for the first time to film *Hang 'Em High*, his first movie since becoming an international star after appearing in the so-called dollar trilogy—*A Fistful of Dollars*, *For a Few Dollars More* and *The Good, the Bad, and the Ugly* (which takes place in New Mexico but was filmed in Spain), all directed by Sergio Leone.

Eastwood's work was shot around Las Cruces and in White Sounds National Monument, which "starred" as Oklahoma and Arkansas. Also appearing in the film were Inger Stevens, famed character actor and former stunt rider Ben Johnson and B-movie cowboy star Bob Steele, who appeared in almost two hundred films during his career. Other recognizable names of the times also had credits in the film, including Alan Hale Jr., who was the Skipper on television's

Clint Eastwood after surviving a near-death experience in *Hang 'Em High*, the first big budget movie shot in southern New Mexico.

Gilligan's Island; Bruce Dern, whose career has included many starring roles and as many small roles; and Dennis Hopper just prior to his success in *Easy Rider*. Hopper called Taos, New Mexico, home for many years.

A smaller role went to L.Q. Jones, one of those actors that you have seen a hundred times but whose name you never know. Jones was so impressed with southern New Mexico that he later tried to start a production company there and also made the small-budget horror film *The Brotherhood of Satan* in the same area in 1971. Jones was the producer and co-star of the picture, which was shot mostly around Hillsboro and Radium Springs, New Mexico, just north and west of Las Cruces.

An interesting anecdote from *Hang 'Em High* comes from Richard Schnickel, the author of *Clint Eastwood*, wherein the director of *Hang 'Em High*, Ted Post, recalled that one of the film's producers, Leonard Freeman (*Hawaii Five-0*), showed up on the set of the movie wearing Cecil B. DeMille–style riding boots and carrying a riding crop, which he would slap against the boots. Eastwood, ever the diplomat (and also a producer), politely took Freeman aside to let him know to stay off the set "or the entire cast and crew would refuse to work."

Things changed shortly thereafter, and a number of production companies rediscovered New Mexico. The year 1969 saw the release of six films that were all shot in part in the state, including the two huge box office hits *Easy Rider* and *Butch Cassidy and the Sundance Kid*.

When the late David Cargo took office as governor on January 1, 1967, it didn't take long for the cameras to really start rolling. That was mostly due to the idea that hatched that made New Mexico the first state in the union to have a film office. The late John Armijo followed the history of the film office during his tenure there and also helped to update the extensive filmography of the state, which became the basis for this book. Armijo wrote:

> Sometime in 1967, newspaper columnist Chuck Mittlestadt and Albuquerque businessman Lou Gasparini had an idea that would bring motion picture and television production to New Mexico. The duo took their idea to [then] Governor David Cargo and without skipping a beat, he formed a committee to work out the details. This paved the way for New Mexico to become the first state in the country to establish a state office whose primary purpose was to promote the state as an incentive to lure the film community to the Land of Enchantment. At the time Cargo was the youngest governor in the United States.
>
> The original name of the office was New Mexico Motion Picture Industries Committee. In 1971, the name was changed to Motion

Dennis Hopper and Peter Fonda, the stars of *Easy Rider*, leaving Taos Pueblo. *Easy Rider* is one of the few films that have received permission from the Taos Pueblo people to film there. *Courtesy of www.movies.nm-unlimited2.net.*

Picture Bureau of the New Mexico Department of Commerce, then in 1980, probably because no one could remember the moniker, and much to the delight of the Graphics Arts Division [of Tourism], the name was changed to New Mexico Film Commission, and in the early 1990s it became the New Mexico Film Office.

The film office was originally housed on the fourth floor at the [state] Round House, but it soon proved to be too distracting for anyone to get any work done with filmmakers signing autographs and posing for pictures, so they moved the office to a less hectic location in downtown Santa Fe. And from there the office moved to 1050 Old Pecos Trail, then to the Joseph Montoya building at the corner of St. Francis Drive and Cordova Road. The film office moved two more times in recent years to return back at the Joseph Montoya building. Whew! It's been a long journey. (The office also had offices for a few years in a space above the then closed Jean Cocteau Cinema, with the idea of opening a state film museum in the theater.)

Newman and Redford as Butch and Sundance in this one-sheet theater poster. *Courtesy of www.impawards.com.*

Not long after the legislature made the original committee a statutory commission, under the umbrella of the New Mexico Department of Development (DOD), members of the committee began a series of telephone calls to Hollywood that went ignored. Committee member [author] *Max Evans volunteered to fly out to Los Angeles, at his own expense, to follow-up on the leads and with the help of his agent, Dick Brand, they began nailing down appointments.*

By the end of 1968, the sales trip to Los Angeles had brought in $40 million in productions and, in 1972, it swelled to $89 million. Not bad for a start-up company staffed by three people. Between 1968 and 1978 a total of 108 film and television productions were produced in New Mexico, and since 1898, the Land of Enchantment has hosted over 800 productions.

In 1969, Butch Cassidy and the Sundance Kid, Easy Rider, The Good Guys and the Bad Guys, Heaven with a Gun, *and* The McMasters *all filmed around the state, as did two Disney features* Hang Your Hat on the Wind *and* Pancho: The Fastest Paw in the West.

One of the first films to shoot in the state as a result of the sales trip to Los Angeles was The Good Guys and the Bad Guys, *directed by Burt Kennedy. In 1998, Kennedy, a good friend of Evans, and a great admirer of everything New Mexico, returned to help celebrate New Mexico's 100 Years of Filmmaking. The gala event was held at the Gerald Peters Art Gallery in Santa Fe.* The Good Guys *cast included Robert Mitchum, George Kennedy, Martin Balsam, David and John Carradine, Tina Louise, Lois Nettleton, and Marie Windsor. The Nitty Gritty Dirt Band also appeared in the film. But the real star of the film was the Cumbres & Toltec Railroad. The narrow gauge train had been in moth balls until it was resurrected by the production company to the tune of $150,000.*

Warner-Seven Arts brought a cast and crew of 150 personnel into Chama and employed a goodly amount of its 1,500 residents, and if they weren't employed as extras they provided services to the production company. It was reported that every motel room in the vicinity was booked solid for six to seven weeks. Even the Tierra Amarilla Escalante High School Band appeared in the picture. The studio was spending $50,000 per week, which included $1,300+ a day for housing and $1,000+ per day being spent on food and restaurants.

The world premiere of The Good Guys and the Bad Guys *was a benefit for the Carrie Tingley Hospital for Crippled Children in Truth or*

The Cumbres and Toltec Railroad—based in Chama, New Mexico—has been used in more than twenty movies and television works since 1968. *Courtesy of the New Mexico Film Office.*

Paul Newman and Robert Redford attempting their great escape in *Butch Cassidy and the Sundance Kid*, which used the Cumbres and Toltec Railroad. *Courtesy of www.movies.nm-unlimited2.net.*

Consequences [formerly Hot Springs], *NM. The premiere was held at the Lensic and El Paseo theaters in Santa Fe. In attendance at both venues were stars George Kennedy, Tina Louise, and Martin Balsam. La Fonda hotel was also the setting for a pre-screening cocktail party and banquet attended by 120 invited guests. The after party was at the governor's mansion. A repeat "world" premiere and benefit was held the next day at the Sunshine Theater in Albuquerque.*

Though New Mexico got into movies before Hollywood, Santa Fe and the rest of New Mexico settled into a fitful supporting role. Our gorgeous scenery and relative proximity to Los Angeles lured directors of westerns and Native American–themed films from the earliest days.

Cargo himself discussed the founding of the nation's first official film commission in his autobiographical book *Lonesome Dave* (2010).

Besides Middlestadt, who was a writer/columnist and also a stringer for the *Hollywood Reporter,* and Gasparini, a theater manager, the commission included artist Fred Harman (co-founder of the famed comic strip *Red Ryder*); writers Evans, Don Hamilton, Dick Skrondahl and Ralph Looney; author Jack Schaefer (*Shane*); Charles Le Maire, who won three Oscars during his career as a costume designer; Jack Stamm; William Previtti, who was Cargo's press secretary; and representatives from Albuquerque's three television stations, KOAT TV (Max Sklower), KOB TV (Jerry Danziger) and KGGM TV (Ernest "Stretch" Scherer). Sadly, Scherer was murdered in 1972 by a mentally ill man.

In a brief interview in 2015, Max Sklower, who has since changed careers from television to real estate, remembered that time fondly, offering, "I loved doing that. I went to Hollywood a couple of times with some of the other committee members and it really helped bring movies to New Mexico. I was the vice-chairman and was on the commission for about five or six years. It was Gasparini who was the head of it at then."

Sklower was also a campaign planner for various political candidates, and he recalled with a smile, "If they didn't listen to me, they lost!"

Cargo writes that it all started very informally after he saw a movie in Albuquerque at a theater managed by Gasparini, who casually mentioned to the governor, "We need to set up a film commission."

The commission couldn't have had a better blend of members, since each had his own area of expertise, with some being connected with the local press and others with Hollywood. Schaefer, who authored *Shane* that the famed movie was based on, had some of those connections, as did Le Maire.

A few months later, Evans and LeMaire tried to set up a meeting between Hollywood-based directors and producers, Cargo and other members of the commission. Evans was pivotal in "cajoling and asking everyone he knew" to help set up or attend the meeting. Evans knew his way around Hollywood a little bit since his book *The Rounders* was made into a contemporary western comedy that starred Glenn Ford and Henry Fonda. That film originally was scheduled to be made near Santa Fe, but circumstances soon found that the picture had to actually shoot in and around Sedona, Arizona.

Cargo and several of the commission members—along with other people who had gotten involved in the idea, including investigative reporter/filmmaker Charlie Cullen (*The Silence of Cricket Coogler*)—attended the meeting, as did some industry supporters like actors Chill Wills (a co-star of *The Rounders*), Robert Montgomery (star and director of *Ride the Pink Horse*) and musician/actor Burl Ives, who had a home near Santa Fe. The meeting consisted of about thirty-five people connected with the film industry; they were shown a short film that had been made by the committee in order to promote itself.

Cargo recalled that "it was probably the worst promo film ever made by anyone, anywhere," but even though it was met with guffawing by the "professionals," it also received thunderous applause. The guests all knew that it was a "primitive piece," but they really felt the sincerity behind what the group was trying to do and that they were doing the best that they could with what they had to work with. They embraced the idea even before Cargo gave a short speech, which Evans later described as "magic." Before the lunch break, the commission had some pretty firm commitments, one by director Burt Kennedy, another from producer Mark Hanna and a third by Oscar Nichols, author Clair Huffaker and producer Jerry Adler. Cargo also met and became friends with Bill Castle of Paramount Pictures, who was riding high at the time due to his success with a number of movies.

A tour of Paramount and Universal Studios also led to the meeting of actor Dan Blocker (*Bonanza*), who had spent some time teaching in Carlsbad, New Mexico. It was a bit embarrassing, since Blocker had done an ad for Cargo's rival in the gubernatorial election, but with a smile, Blocker offered his vote "next time" if Cargo ran again and if Blocker returned to New Mexico.

Cargo also met with various union officers during the trip, which became a very important introduction since "unions purposely sent films to [be made in] New Mexico whenever they could."

Evans, Cargo and his wife, Ida Jo, made additional trips to Tinseltown, paying their own way since the commission didn't have a budget at that time. Later, state lawmakers did provide an initial budget of $30,000, which was later raised to $100,000 during Cargo's last year in office. Cargo further stated that $3.5 billion came to New Mexico via film projects during those early years and accurately notes that almost every state has a film office now and that many of New Mexico's larger communities sport film liaisons or, in some cases, such as Santa Fe and Albuquerque, film offices.

And then, as now, some state legislators failed to see the financial impact of movie shoots in the state, as one state representative wanted the budget sliced by $60,000 and others didn't want to fund the commission at all. Representative Tom Hoover claimed that Cargo was laughably trying "to further his own career in films." The measure was soundly defeated after several hours of debate on the floor of the state House of Representatives. The commission was placed under the auspices of the state's Department of Development.

Perhaps Hoover wised up a bit later when Kennedy filmed his western comedy *The Good Guys and the Bad Guys* around the town of Chama, reviving the dormant Cumbres and Toltec Railroad, part of which was used for a down payment to buy the railroad for New Mexico and Colorado, which is where it operates as a tourist attraction even today.

In an article in *Santa Fean Magazine*, New Mexico native and longtime film producer Alton Walpole added, "That was a pretty major thing at the time. They actually established an office to help producers who came in and had no idea what they were walking into. They really don't have much idea what's here. *Crazy Heart* was written for Texas, but the producers just looked around the Southwest and decided this was the best place to be."

Walpole worked on the 2010 Oscar-nominated film *Crazy Heart* as a line producer and more recently with *Beyond the Reach* (2015), with Michael Douglas. (A line producer manages the day-to-day operations of a film.)

Kaaren Ochoa is also quoted in that piece. Ochoa was first assistant director and said, "After filming *Beyond the Reach*, I heard [actor] Michael Douglas tell the crew, 'I've worked in L.A. and New York and all over the world and you put those crews to shame.' And he meant it! Those kinds of things are important regarding what the incentives accomplished."

These are strong reasons films are so often shot in the state nowadays—the availability, accessibility and competence of the trained crews that are available to work with.

Karen Koch—a producer whose résumé includes work on several New Mexico films including *Spoken Word* (2009) and *50 to 1* (2013)—shared, "New Mexico went from location-dependent to rebate-dependent today.

That is the simple story here. The rebate has created movies that can use the landscape as opposed to the landscape being the critical factor."

Recent years have seen debate and several conflicting studies about New Mexico's film incentive program. Filmmakers benefit by skipping gross-receipts taxes and receiving a 25 percent tax rebate for production expenditures. Albuquerque was recently ranked the number-one place to shoot a film by *MovieMaker Magazine*. For the last few years, lawmakers in Santa Fe have introduced bills to limit the incentive program. As expected, most of the bills are introduced by legislators who represent parts of the state that see little if any of this cash cow. As a column in the *Farmington Daily Herald* asked, "What about us?" Representative Dennis Kintigh from Roswell maintained that film incentives *cost* the state more than $80 million in 2014. One study by accounting firm Ernst and Young showed that thirty films in New Mexico in 2007 generated more than $250 million in spending. But another study, one from New Mexico State University of all places, concluded the state nets less than fifteen cents for every dollar spent on the film industry. Political infighting aside, the film industry remains vigorous throughout New Mexico.

But it didn't take long for Governor Cargo to catch on to how things sometimes work in the film industry. One of the things that he did to get filmmakers to consider New Mexico as a shooting location was to find out that a movie was being shot in a different state. He would then call one of the cast or crew members, causing things to come to a halt on that production since everyone would hear that the governor's office was calling. He'd get his prey on the phone, talking to him or her in convincing terms and try to have that production moved to New Mexico. The state had also set a pay scale of sixteen dollars a day for extras, compared to the Hollywood rate of thirty-six to fifty-five dollars. And the commission bent over backwards to help get whatever a crew needed, from old cars to old cows.

Armijo found that by the end of 1968, the fledgling office, then staffed by only three people (which is now oddly staffed only by four, even with record production taking place in the state as this book goes to press), had brought in $40 million. By 1972, it was close to $90 million that helped to fill the state treasury.

It appears that Phillip St. George Cooke was the first film historian in the state, but records are not clear about whether he was a volunteer or a paid staff member. He also produced a series of pamphlet-style historical magazines called *New Mexico Territorial* around this time. Cooke made many efforts to establish the state's first filmography and apparently also tried to gather copies of films made in New Mexico, as indicated by records found in the state archives. Cooke wrote to studios and stars as he tried to compile a list of movies, which was later updated by John Armijo and others, myself included.

A letter dated April 1970 from actress Lillian Gish to Cooke notes that she wished that she "had made a picture in your land of enchantment" after his query to her to see if she had done work in New Mexico.

Another correspondence to Cooke is a bit of a mystery, since it is from Warner Brothers/Seven Arts and notes that producer Phil Feldman (*The Wild Bunch*), an associate of director Sam Peckinpah, had spoken with Leo Wilder of Warner Brothers and "assured me that upon distribution tabling of Max Evans' book, Warner Brothers is in a position to do major promotion."

This may refer to Evans's book *The Hi-Lo Country*, which was optioned several times by Peckinpah, who really wanted to do a film of Evans's excellent volume. Peckinpah was unable to do so, but in 1998, English director Stephen Frears did ("I've always wanted to make a western"). The contemporary drama starred Woody Harrelson and Patricia Arquette. Although the picture failed due to the bankruptcy of the distributor, Gramercy, the film is eloquent and strong and uses the landscapes of northern and northeast New Mexico to strong advantage.

One other letter from Warner Brothers Studios dated November 24, 1969, notes that two films about New Mexico, *Raton Pass* (1951) and *Santa Fe Trail* (1940), premiered here (a very small part of Raton Pass, perhaps an insert shot, appears in the film, while *Santa Fe Trail* was never even close to the state line for filming purposes), and that two other pictures, *Strange Lady in Town* (1955) and *The Left Handed Gun* (1958), were both set in the state but not filmed here. It was later proven that the latter had some second unit shooting done near Santa Fe.

Warner's indicates that seven of its productions were shot at least in part in New Mexico, including *The Desert Song* (1942); *Pursued* (1946); *Rocky Mountain* (1950); *A Distant Trumpet* (1963); *A Covenant with Death* (1966); the often mentioned *The Good Guys and the Bad Guys* (1969), for which star Robert Mitchum stated years later that "he was sorry he did the picture"; and *Nobody Loves Flapping Eagle* (1969), which received a merciful title change to *Flap* before release. The original title was the name of the novel that the film was based on, which was supposedly to be "for" the rights of American Indians but instead comes off as a rather embarrassing piece. In the film, Anthony Quinn, who is of Mexican descent, stars as Flap with other actors again appearing in "red face."

Cargo indicates in his book that *Flap* needed a title change and that he "remonstrated" to Warner's that the title was inappropriate. They made the change and held a special premiere of the film in Albuquerque, where much of the film was made, with Quinn as a special guest. To help cover its faux pas, the studio also made all proceeds from the showing available as part of a $75,000 scholarship to be used by American Indians who wanted to try for a career in the creative arts, "including cinema."

The film is steadfastly awful, even though it was directed by Carol Reed, who made several outstanding pictures prior, including the Oscar-winning *Oliver* and the highly regarded film noir *The Third Man*. Another curiosity about the picture is that Richard Harris was supposed to star rather than Quinn but withdrew because of "creative differences." That was probably a good idea.

Cooke also cleared up some confusion about another film that was in production at the time—*Chisum*, with John Wayne—which was actually shot around Durango, Mexico, and not in New Mexico, even though the real Chisum was a very historical name during the cattle drive years in the late 1800s. Chisum had a huge ranch in southeastern New Mexico and was one of the parties responsible for the hiring of Pat Garrett as a lawman, who later killed the infamous Billy the Kid.

Cargo wrote in his book that he also advocated for filmmakers to be made exempt from the states gross receipts and inventory taxes, something that he proudly saw come into law on July 1, 1970.

5

REDISCOVERED!

The Cargo Years

With the opening of the film office and the tiny full-time staff to help filmmakers large and small find their way around the state, moviemaking in New Mexico became a huge industry for the state in the '70s. To this day, many people don't "get it"; they feel that the film companies just come here to take advantage of the incentive programs and tax breaks.

Certainly that is part of the equation, but naysayers fail to take into consideration that when a film company is in New Mexico, everyone with said company needs somewhere to sleep, somewhere to eat, transportation to get them from point A to point B and a number of other things that go along with daily life. They don't just spend all of their time on the movie set.

Some of the bigger names that were in New Mexico during this period include Jimmy Stewart and Henry Fonda in *The Cheyenne Social Club* (1970), a picture that allows New Mexico to "star" as Texas, Oklahoma and Wyoming, as the two actors play itinerant cowboys on their way to Cheyenne, Wyoming, to collect Stewart's inheritance, a bordello, in this western comedy. This might be the only time that a movie with that sort of business as part of the story ever received a G rating. It is also honored by Fonda's "singing" debut in a picture, which is not overly memorable. Much of the film was shot around Santa Fe.

Fonda returned, albeit briefly, to the state to film part of *There Was a Crooked Man* (1970) near La Joya, New Mexico, north of the town of Socorro. Again, it is hard to define just what part of the picture was shot there and why, and that may be lost to history.

The McMasters, another western, is said to be the first film shot entirely in New Mexico. The film's interior shots were done at the state's first sound stage, called the Film Center, located at the Santa Fe National Guard Armory.

Utilizing the then ghost town of Madrid, New Mexico, and the surrounding environment—including the village of Galisteo and the Tesuque and San Ildefonso Pueblos—this tight little picture was financed by an English filmmaking company and has as its stars Brock Peters, Burl Ives and Jack Palance. Nancy Kwan and David Carradine sadly star as Native Americans; neither of them is of American Indian descent. It is a dark tale, replete with rampant racism shown toward Peters, who plays a black Union soldier returning from the Civil War enduring some violence, both physical and emotional. Although it did not do well at the box office, it made its way into New Mexico film history by being the first "all New Mexico" feature film.

Plenty of offbeat pictures were shot at least partially in New Mexico during the '70s as well, including *Gas-s-s-s*, directed by B movie king Roger Corman. The film is a product of the times, one could say, wherein a nerve gas is released in Alaska that is meant to kill anyone over twenty-five. Comedic anarchy ensues, most of it in New Mexico, including the Acoma Pueblo, Socorro, Belen, Albuquerque and even Grants, a small city west of Albuquerque.

Another genuine curio and the first feature film shot entirely in Las Cruces is *Up in the Cellar*. Directed by Theodore J. Flicker, who also did a few other comedic low-budget pictures before becoming a sculptor in Santa Fe. *Up in the Cellar* was a parody of sorts of *Three in the Attic*, a very popular film of the times. It stars Wes Stern (yes, that was his name) and future superstars Larry Hagman (*Dallas*) and Joan Collins of *Dynasty* fame. Stern plays a college student who gets revenge on the university president by bedding the president's wife and his daughter (and assorted others along the way) after his scholarship is rejected. Several interesting stories about this film have come out since research began on this project.

One was from director Flicker himself, who screened the film in Las Cruces as a thank-you for the community's help while shooting the picture. The theater was full, and no one really knew what the film was about other than it was a comedy and that much of it had been shot on the New Mexico State University campus. The elderly guests in the audience also didn't know that it contained a scene with a young actress baring her breasts during the screening of a student film that took place in the movie. Flicker told me that when that scene came on, he heard more gasps and saw more people head for the exit door than during any other movie ever.

David Cargo, who had a bit part in the film, was in California when the film was released and happened by a theater one day that listed his name on the marquee. But along with that was the notation that the movie was rated X (although it was only an R movie). The governor immediately contacted Flicker to ensure that his name would not be posted on other marquees.

There may have been X-rated movies shot within the state boundaries, but a brief search for them came up with nothing, other than an incorrect notation on IMDB.com that a Swedish crew once shot an explicit film about

Warren Oates and Peter Fonda in *The Hired Hand,* the best western ever made in New Mexico. *Courtesy of Western Clippings and Boyd Magers.*

lesbian lovers who worked in a Santa Fe laundry, which proved to be false. The director told me via e-mail he had never even been to New Mexico.

The other aside of note is that Flicker was also able to shoot the partial demolition of downtown Las Cruces, which was undergoing a poorly planned urban renewal project that the city has still—more than forty years later—never recovered from.

The year 1971 remains one of the biggest ever for number of films shot in New Mexico, with nearly twenty movies making their screen debut that year. Among them is probably the best western ever shot in the state, *The Hired Hand*, directed by and starring Peter Fonda in his first film since *Easy Rider*. Allegorical and beautifully shot, with a cast that includes character actor Warren Oates and Verna Bloom, the film is an atmospheric western that remains unparalleled in the genre.

The picture was shot mostly in northern New Mexico, around Chama and the almost ghost town of Cabezon, with some work being done at White Sands National Monument and near Espanola and Alamogordo, New Mexico, as well. Only a few "in town" shots were done in Hollywood.

The film received negative reviews for the most part and was booked in only fifty-two theaters upon its first release and then shelved after a two-week run. The film languished for years until it was rediscovered by famed producer/director Martin Scorsese. Then, it was restored in time for another release to several film festivals in 2001–2 before a small general release to art house venues in 2003. It cost only $820,000 to make and should be noted as a classic of the western genre.

What has become a true cult or underground film—which could be interpreted as you love it or hate it—is the '71 release *Two-Lane Blacktop*. It was directed by Monte Hellman, whose career has been scattered and unique—running the gamut of film genres from esoteric westerns *The Shooting* and *Ride the Whirlwind*, both of which star Jack Nicholson, to low-budget horror films like *Silent Night, Deadly Night III* (1989) to other art films including *Cockfighter* (1974) and *Iguana* (1988).

But *Two-Lane* trumps them all. (I love this film, so expect bias for the next several paragraphs.) The story involves two young men, singer James Taylor in his first and only film (supposedly he did not watch the film until 2009) and the late Dennis Wilson of the surf rock band the Beach Boys. This was Wilson's only appearance in a movie as well.

It is said that Al Pacino, Robert DeNiro, Jon Voight and Michael Sarrazin were all considered for the part of the Driver, the role that went to Taylor after Hellman saw a picture of him on a billboard in Los Angeles. The role of GTO was offered to Bruce Dern and Kris Kristofferson, both of whom declined. Wilson is the Mechanic.

Aimless and pretty much living in their stripped-down but plenty fast '55 Chevy, the two men live by challenging other street racers for money. However, that changes when they are challenged by another driver, "GTO," a pathological liar played flawlessly by the late, great character actor Warren Oates. Soon the two cars are on a west–east cross-country road race, with the winner receiving the pink slip (title) of the other's car.

Each car encounters several unusual characters as the race proceeds, with little dialogue and absolutely no change in expression from Taylor. The Girl, played by Laurie Bird, just gets in the Chevy one day while the two men are stopped at a diner and accompanies them part way on the trip, which includes stops in several locations in Santa Fe and at the former Ute gas station in Tucumcari, New Mexico.

The whole thing might seem pointless and dull, but if viewers are able to inject their own emotions and observe the emptiness and loneliness of the Driver, the Mechanic, GTO and the Girl, the film plays out very well. And we won't spoil it for you by telling you about the remarkable ending.

Funnily enough, the same '55 Chevy was a co-star in *American Graffiti*, filmed two years later. There were three customized Chevys made for the film, with the last surviving one selling at auction in 2015 for $159,500.

One scene was filmed at Bert's Burger Bowl in Santa Fe, which, to the dismay of locals, closed in early 2015. As I drove by it one day shortly after it closed, an exact replica of the '55 Chevy was in the parking lot with three very sad occupants who were going cross-country to retrace the route taken in the movie. They had missed having a famed green chile cheeseburger at Bert's by about a month.

And sadly, Bird—who later became the girlfriend of singer/poet Art Garfunkel and who had been involved with Hellman as well—committed suicide in 1979.

Many of the other films of that year were smaller in nature and now are mostly forgotten. One of those was the made-for-television, Italian-produced piece, *Ripped Off*, which also had four other titles, including *The Boxer*. Ernest Borgnine and Robert Blake starred in the picture.

The film was one of a handful of internationally produced films that took place in the state during those years. Others were the Spanish/Mexican–financed film *Temporada Salvaje (The Wild Season)*, with Diane McBain of the popular television show *The Avengers*; *The Man With the Icy Eyes*, also from an Italian filmmaking crew; and *Medicine Ball Caravan*, a documentary that followed a traveling music festival across the country, with a stop in Placitas, New Mexico, just north of Albuquerque.

Medicine Ball Caravan was created by a bevy of Frenchmen hired by the big Warner Brothers Studios. Warner also hired 154 "hippies" to travel from San Francisco to Washington, D.C., to help spread the word about what the studio publicists called the "Aquarian Lifestyle" using a number of free concerts along the way to do so.

Although $1 million was spent, it wasn't done wisely, as the intended young audience stayed away from the theaters hosting the film, with *Rolling Stone* magazine naming it one of the ten worst films of the year.

The idea for *Medicine Ball Caravan* took place after the hugely successful Woodstock festival and was seen as a sort of Woodstock on wheels. Even with such performers as Alice Cooper; Doug Kershaw of Cajun music fame; the world-famous B.B. King, whose Placitas performance is one of the few scenes that is accessible (via YouTube); and the (then) very popular band Hot Tuna, by the time the picture was released in August 1971, the whole idea of long hair, beads and partial nudity had become far out but not in a good way. A title change to *We Have Come for Your Daughters*, a slogan painted on one of the buses in the caravan, was for naught as well. The movie tanked and is hard to find in any format.

Made-for-television pieces, including two episodes of *Bearcats!*, and a couple other documentaries were also shot around the state in the '70s, along with several westerns, such as *Shoot Out*, with Gregory Peck, and *A Gunfight*, which is one of the first movies to have two endings and perhaps the first to be sponsored by an American Indian tribe, the Jicarilla Apaches, as well as the one and only to star both Kirk Douglas and Johnny Cash. However, two of the other films shot in New Mexico during this period do stand out among those sadly forgotten productions: *Billy Jack* and *Red Sky at Morning*.

Billy Jack—which was produced by, directed by and starred a then little-known actor named Tom Laughlin—shook up the studios. With a budget of less than $1 million, Laughlin and crew—including his wife, Delores Taylor—made an iconic picture that has brought in over $200 million since its release. The film was mostly shot in and around Santa Fe, made a star of Laughlin and changed the way that films are booked into theaters. After many deals and broken promises from studios, Laughlin eventually did his own distribution, opening the film in a number of theaters at once, an unheard-of practice at the time. He made two other *Billy Jack* features and started a third, which stopped production due to funding issues.

Actor Keenan Wynn (l) takes a break on the set of the 1971 television series *Bearcats!* *Courtesy of John Armijo.*

Bearcats!, a one-season wonder, incorporated the Old West with upcoming changes such as cars in this witty and well-written series. *Courtesy of John Armijo.*

Unexpectedly, Laughlin also worked on an idea that would have been the grandparent of Netflix. His intention was to set up a network of neighborhood distributors who would have the country's largest catalogue of videotapes on hand and have the cassettes rented and delivered by people who worked for the neighborhood distributors. Brilliant!

Red Sky at Morning, on the other hand, remains a little-seen film unless you happen to catch it on cable TV, since it has never been officially released on DVD or even VHS. Based on a novel by Santa Fe resident Richard Bradford, who later gave up writing, the film was also shot mostly in the Santa Fe area. It stars Richard Thomas, the star of the television show *The Waltons*; Desi Arnaz Jr., who won a Golden Globe Award for Most Promising (Male) Newcomer; and Cathy Burns, who gave up the acting business a few years later.

The film is a very authentic coming-of-age tale, with Thomas moving to New Mexico from Alabama during World War II when his father is called to active duty in the U.S. Navy. The picture takes an interesting look at different aspects of life in New Mexico. Perhaps not overly piquant today, during the time the film was made, when the whole country had to embrace different cultures, the film at least made a mild attempt to show how Chicanos were treated during that time.

The next year, 1972, notes an amazing number of New Mexico productions as well, numbering sixteen, with most of them smaller films, sometimes with big-name actors. Among those actors was Charlton Heston, who appeared in *Skyjacked*, which used the Albuquerque airport for a scene depicting a Russian military base.

The film later had to go through some legal wrangling, partially because it was thought it would scare potential airline passengers since it was released during a time when skyjacking planes was in vogue for malcontents of all kinds. It also touches on what is now known as post-traumatic stress disorder, with James Brolin co-starring as an afflicted Vietnam vet.

Paul Newman and Lee Marvin were also part of the motion picture scene during this year. They starred in a modern-day western comedy called *Pocket Money*. An almost intolerably dull film, it was partly filmed around Santa Fe, and famed director Terrence Malick *(Days of Heaven, The Thin Red Line)* was part of the crew.

Since there is little mention of the filmmaking industry in the New Mexico state archives, one has to assume it was through the efforts of Governor Cargo and others who helped get the word out about the state's lush landscapes and helpful attitudes that brought so many productions here.

Even some stars who were slightly past their prime ended up here in low-budget productions, including Bette Davis and Ernest Borgnine, both former Academy Award winners, who co-starred in a lowball comedy called *Bunny O'Hare*, which was almost released as *Bunny and Claude*.

Filming principally in New Mexico, in and around Albuquerque and points south including the towns of Los Lunas and Belen, the film was not well received. It is a gentle comedy, somewhat farcical, featuring the two stars as elderly bank robbers who often disguise as "hippies." Davis later sued American International Pictures, alleging that it had changed the script to "slapstick" from what she was told would be a "humorous social commentary" picture.

Cargo himself has a cameo in this film, one of several that you can catch a glimpse of him in, including *Up in the Cellar*, *The Good Guys and the Bad Guys*, *The Gatling Gun*, *The Boxer* and *Convoy*.

Molly and Lawless John is one of the first westerns ever filmed from a woman's point of view. A feminist western, it stars Vera Miles as Molly and was one of the first feature films to use locations all over the state. The film uses locations from southern New Mexico, in the Las Cruces and Mesilla area (using the famous La Posta Restaurant as a house of ill repute), to the White Sands National Monument to the Cerrillos and Pecos area near Santa Fe.

Made-for-television movies also continued to come to New Mexico to roost, including *Gargoyles*, which starred another actor in need of a career boost, Cornel Wilde. Wilde plays a scientist in the film, which was shot around Carlsbad and at Carlsbad Caverns National Park. Wilde and his daughter, played by Jennifer Salt, stumble on the creatures, and Salt's character almost loses her top to a jealous female gargoyle. Shot with only one camera, it was reported that the temperature hovered around one hundred degrees during the three weeks of filming.

Two other notable westerns for the year are *The Honkers* and *The Cowboys*. *The Honkers* is a modern-day western also shot around Carlsbad, featuring James Coburn as an arrogant and womanizing rodeo star and former New Mexico resident Slim Pickens as his sometimes savior. *The Cowboys* is the only film shot in New Mexico that clearly shows that John Wayne was, at one time, our guest. Wayne's other works that used New Mexico as a home base, albeit briefly, are the previously mentioned *The Flying Tigers* and *Without Reservations*.

But *The Cowboys* became famous for things besides being shot in the land of enchantment. Using the parched areas around Santa Fe as Montana and South Dakota, Wayne plays rancher Wil Anderson, whose entire crew of cowhands quits to go look for gold after a gold strike. Left without help before his yearly cattle drive, Wayne is forced to hire a bunch of local boys to work as cowboys. Jebediah Nightlinger (a superb turn by Roscoe Lee Browne) is the camp cook and the only other adult on the trip.

Soon Long Hair (Bruce Dern at his evilest) and his cohorts arrive on the scene asking for jobs. Anderson catches Long Hair in a lie after he says that they rode herd for another rancher who has been dead for years. He turns them away only to find that his herd has now become the goal of Long Hair and his band of rustlers.

This is one of the few films in which Wayne meets his demise. There are said to be seven in all, including *The Shootist*, *The Alamo* and *Sands of Iwo Jima*.

Director Mark Rydell wanted George C. Scott for Wayne's role because of his distaste for Wayne's political views (one wonders if Long Hair was the ultimate bad guy on purpose), but that didn't pan out. Politics had to be held at bay between Wayne and Browne as well, although they found common ground through their interest in poetry. Dern, who shoots Wayne in what is the only film where we see a main character kill the Duke, received death threats after the movie's release. Others who've dispatched Wayne over the years include a giant squid in *Reap the Wild Wind*; snipers in *The Alamo*, *Iwo Jima* and *The Fighting Seabees*; a barkeep in *The Shootist*; and via shipwreck in *Wake of the Red Witch*.

After Cargo left office, the number of films shot in New Mexico started to slip. In 1973 and '74, production and quality took a serious decline, resulting in only twenty known productions in the state, many of which were made for network television or were only in state to do part of a shoot.

Many westerns were made, most of which were smaller-budget films such as *Running Wild* with Lloyd Bridges; *Santee*, which stars Glenn Ford; and *The Gatling Gun*. It was up to Rock Hudson and Dean Martin to add slightly bigger names to the mix when they appeared in *Showdown*, which was shot mostly in northern New Mexico using the Cumbres and Toltec Railroad, which is based in Chama, and the scenery around Abiquiu, the longtime home of famed artist Georgia O'Keeffe. It is also one of the few films that have been able to utilize a real forest fire for an action scene.

The network movies included *Nakia* and the ensuing television series and *Born Innocent*, starring Linda Blair, who made a name for herself in *The Exorcist*.

One interesting aspect of filmmaking during this time relates to the number of films that were made in the state by African American filmmakers. *The Legend of Nigger Charley* was among the first of this small surge, with the real title including the n-word, although *Black* was substituted when the picture played on television. The movie was shot mostly in the Santa Fe area.

The picture stars former NFL player Fred Williamson, who stepped in after distinguished character actor Woody Strode pulled out of the production. The film is a western wherein Charley, born into slavery, and two companions escape from a plantation after killing a man. They head west, and adventures and violence ensues. The picture took a drubbing by critics but was a money-making hit for audiences, which were estimated to be 90 percent African American.

It spawned a sequel, *The Soul of Nigger Charley*, and a spate of other low-budget productions, including *Adios Amigo*, a western comedy with Williamson and Richard Pryor, who improvised most of his lines; *Boss Nigger*, another western starring Williamson; *The Take*, which showcased Billy Dee Williams; *Black Connection* (aka *Run, Nigger, Run*); and a true oddity, *Thomasine and Bushrod*, which is kind of a mix of Bonnie and Clyde and Robin Hood. All of these films were shot at least in part in the Albuquerque/Santa Fe area.

Thomasine and Bushrod was directed by Gordon Parks Jr., probably making the film the first ever New Mexico–made movie that was directed by a black artist. It did pretty well at the box office, with most patrons again said to be African American, so New Mexico can lay claim to the fact that it helped black directors and cast members find their footing in the highly competitive industry of moviemaking.

Another film made during this time was *Catch My Soul*, labeled a "rock and roll version of *Othello*," one of William Shakespeare's better-known works. Musician Richie Havens stars in the title role, and Patrick McGoohan (*The Prisoner*, *Secret Agent*) directed, his only effort for a feature film. At the time, McGoohan was living in Santa Fe after leaving the United Kingdom. There were about 150 Santa Fe locals used in the production, and when the picture tanked at the box office, it was retitled *Santa Fe Satan*, which didn't help one bit.

One of 1973's most unique films, based on a bestselling book of the times, also has a brief New Mexico connection. *Jonathan Livingston Seagull*, the story of a woefully dissatisfied seagull who goes on a journey of discovery, has a brief scene that was shot, or perhaps superimposed, into Carlsbad Caverns. The film was not well received, not even by the author of the volume himself, Richard Bach. It is also listed as one of the few movies that famed film critic Roger Ebert ever walked out of.

Linda Blair, the young actress who achieved fame for her performance in *The Exorcist*, did come to our fair state for two made-for-television movies.

Born Innocent was the first, in which she plays a young reform school girl. The picture was shot in Albuquerque and also in nearby Algodones, New Mexico. Blair returned to New Mexico a couple years later to shoot another television production with Martin Sheen, *Sweet Hostage*. Taos, New Mexico, was the location, with Blair playing an illiterate girl from a rural community who is kidnapped by mountain man Sheen.

Nakia, starring Robert Forster as a Native American lawman (even though he is not Native American), had a one-season television run, going for fourteen episodes. It was shot in the Albuquerque area. To the series' credit, it was the first television series to depict an American Indian in a contemporary setting. It is too bad that the producers didn't have the common sense to use a real Native American actor.

The years 1975 to '77 saw about the same number of productions as '73 and '74, with twenty-one productions being shot at least partially in the state. Most of these works were small-budget pieces, such as *Sidewinder I* and the unforgettable *The Worm Eaters*.

Several large-budget productions found their way around the state, including a western called *Bite the Bullet*. Featuring an all-star cast that included Gene Hackman, Candice Bergen and James Coburn, the film utilized several parts of New Mexico, including White Sands National Monument; the Carson National Forest near Taos, New Mexico; and the Cumbres and Toltec Railroad at Chama. It was a box office hit, earning $7 million, which was remarkable for a western during those times.

Warren Beatty, Jack Nicholson and Stockard Channing made a brief appearance in the Santa Fe area in 1975 for one scene of the comedy *The Fortune*, which is somewhat similar in story to the much more famous *The Sting*. The latter starred Paul Newman and current part-time New Mexico resident Robert Redford.

It could be hard to prove, but the 1976 release *The Man Who Fell to Earth*, which stars rock icon David Bowie and Rip Torn, probably holds the record for the most nudity in any New Mexico–made movie. Both stars and several other players bare all for the camera in a film that was shot mostly in southern New Mexico, part of which was shot at White Sands National Monument.

Oddly, it is about an alien (Bowie) who comes to Earth to search for water for his planet and ends up becoming enamored of the capitalist way of life. The picture is the first since 1931 that uses the town of Artesia as part of its backdrop (*The Honkers* from 1972 might have a scene or two shot in Artesia, but it is hard to tell). Even odder is the fact that

Bowie's character is looking for water in one of the most parched states of the Union.

In *100 Years of Filmmaking in New Mexico* (1998), Nicholas Roeg, the director of the film, is quoted as saying, "Every foreigner has their picture of the United States and it doesn't necessarily, well, it hardly ever, envisages New Mexico. After seeing the extraordinary landscape of the White Sands, it prompted me to think of this: strangers always see something that is unfamiliar, you know?"

He was also pleased with the idea that there were a "lot of different places that were quite at hand" while filming here. The cast and crew even worked with the First Presbyterian Church in Artesia, which offered church members as extras and the church itself as a location. After the shoot, which took several hours, the congregation served the crew lunch.

The Missouri Breaks, another western, starred Marlon Brando and Jack Nicholson. It briefly features New Mexico in a few shots done around Taos and at Chama's Cumbres and Toltec Railroad. Tensions were high during the shoot as it was reported that the two stars took an instant dislike to each other.

The only other film of note that has a New Mexico connection during this time—unless you are a fan of *Search for the Gods* (Taos, 1975) or the truly dreadful *Track of the Moonbeast* (1976)—was *Sorcerer* (1977).

Although New Mexico was only on screen for a few minutes, with the Bisti Badlands area near Farmington starring as a desolate spot in South America, this unheralded film should be seen as a classic thriller/adventure film in spite of its poor choice of title. In the film, Roy Scheider, fresh off his starring role in *Jaws*, teams with director William Friedkin, whose star had truly risen after his direction of *The Exorcist*, in a film that has four wanted men driving explosives through the South American jungle to an oil well fire while being watched by bandits and revolutionaries. *Sorcerer* is actually the name of one of the trucks used in the adventure. It is a loose remake of a similarly gripping French film, *Wages of Fear*.

In the book *The Friedkin Connection: A Memoir*, Friedkin offers this as a reason for shooting the end of the film in New Mexico. "It was the landscape we chose for the end of the journey, in which Scanlon (Scheider) embraces madness, abandons his truck, and carries the dynamite two miles to the burning oilfield," he said.

The film was a box office failure, released just before *Star Wars*, but has been reconsidered over the years by audiences and critics alike.

The end of the decade found New Mexico as a still popular destination for filmmakers and studios, but again, many shoots were for smaller films such as *Nightwing*, a silly sci-fi movie in which Italian actor Nick Mancuso stars as an American Indian lawman investigating the appearance of killer bats that attack people. Arthur Hiller, who had made numerous box office hits such as *Love Story* (1970) and *The Hospital* (1971), directed this oddity, which was shot in and around Albuquerque, Santa Fe and the small town of Cubero. Hiller also directed several episodes of the television series *Empire* in New Mexico in the early 1960s. One critical reviewer of *Nightwing* offered, "A film-maker who has made a specialty of showing reverence for platitudes has no jurisdiction over a piece of schlock nonsense about bat-killers in the Arizona desert." And please note that New Mexico "stars" as Arizona in this movie.

There were several good movies and one very bad movie with a big-name star that took root in New Mexico in 1978–79. Clint Eastwood returned to the Land of Enchantment to shoot a small portion of one of his amazingly popular films where he co-stars with an orangutan, *Every Which Way but Loose*. The film has scenes shot in northern New Mexico, including Santa Fe, Taos and Albuquerque.

Convoy, directed by Sam Peckinpah (*The Wild Bunch*, 1969; *Pat Garrett and Billy the Kid*, 1973), was considered by the director to be his worst film but was his biggest box office hit. Based on a novelty song of the same name, performed by former ad executive C.W. McCall (William Dale Fries Jr.), the movie capitalizes on the then popular citizen band (CB) radios and features Kris Kristofferson as an outlaw trucker being pursued by a crazed sheriff, played by Ernest Borgnine. Santa Fe resident Ali MacGraw (*Love Story*, *The Getaway*) plays a love interest of sorts, as eighteen-wheel trucks trash the landscape during numerous chases throughout New Mexico, from White Sands to Las Vegas.

Even the Muppets and Superman have been to New Mexico, with the latter (played by Christopher Reeve) appearing in a scene shot in what is now known as Superman Canyon just outside Gallup, New Mexico. In said scene, the Man of Steel once again rescues Lois Lane, this time just before her stalled car is crushed by earth movements caused by an earthquake.

The Muppets, in their first feature film, *The Muppets Movie*, stop briefly in Albuquerque during their trek to Hollywood in an attempt to get Kermit the Frog into the movies. Chaos ensues.

In all, the 1970s continued the success of the '60s in terms of film productions that visited New Mexico, even if only for a short time. This, however, did not foreshadow the lack of movies made in state in the early 1980s.

6

SLOW AND STEADY

The 1980s and 1990s

W hat do O.J. Simpson, Lee Marvin, Charles Bronson, Sylvia Kristel, Bette Midler, Arnold Schwarzenegger and John Cleese have in common? At one time or another, they appeared in movies that were filmed at least in part in New Mexico during the 1980s.

You may wonder most about Kristel, who was from the Netherlands and made her fame by starring in a series of films based on the sexual adventures of the title character Emmanuelle. In 1981, Kristel was in the Phoenix area shooting a film called *Private Lessons*, which is about the sexual awakening of a young man via Kristel's character, Mallow, a member of the household staff. In the slightly naughty film, Mallow fakes her own death with the help of the young man in order to blackmail the family chauffeur. The film contains several soft sex scenes, and since the age of consent in Arizona was eighteen and the age of consent in New Mexico was only sixteen, the private lessons that star Phillip received from Mallow were shot in Albuquerque, New Mexico.

Lee Marvin and Charles Bronson starred in the film *Death Hunt*, which is loosely based on the true story of "The Mad Trapper" Albert Johnson (whose real name is still not known) during the manhunt for him that took place in the early 1930s. Johnson eluded the Royal Canadian Mounted Police for over a month before being shot at a place on the Eagle River after traveling nearly one hundred miles in the Canadian Arctic during winter. The manhunt was also the first time that an airplane was used to find a fugitive. The film is quite fictional and essentially only uses the main part of

The Governator comes to New Mexico. Arnold Schwarzenegger starred in *The Last Stand*. *Courtesy of Lionsgate.*

the story in the film. The Sandia Mountains on the east side of Albuquerque "star" as Canada in this exciting but dark film.

Schwarzenegger was also in Santa Fe to film *Twins* with co-star Danny DeVito. The story is about one twin searching for the other and, of course, relies heavily on the size difference between the two stars, with Schwarzenegger checking in at six feet two inches and DeVito standing tall at five feet even.

John Cleese, formerly of Monty Python, shows up in the western comedy/drama *Silverado* as a sheriff. The film was directed by Lawrence Kasdan and was very successful at the box office and with critics. It stars a young Kevin Costner, along with Danny Glover, Scott Glenn and Kevin Kline. It is a sort of homage to the westerns of long ago, with a goodly amount of comedy tossed in.

And then there was O.J. Simpson. He had a career in movies after his football career ended and prior to his time as a criminal. He has thirty-four acting credits to his name, much of it in television, including the shot in New Mexico telemovie *Detour to Terror* in which he plays a tourist bus driver who runs into trouble while hauling a group to Las Vegas, Nevada.

Simpson's passengers are harassed and threatened by three nutcases on dune buggies, who are after one of the bus's passengers that they mistakenly think is a woman of wealth and good fortune. Interesting, in a way, is the fact that Nicole Brown Simpson also has a small part in the film, which was shot in the Albuquerque area. The film was also produced by Simpson and by *Playboy* magazine.

The '80s brought a fair number of other productions to New Mexico as well. From 1980 to '82, the state hosted sixteen productions. Few were groundbreaking and many were made for television, including *Detour to Terror*; the superb *Ballad of Gregorio Cortez*, which was based on a true story and shot around Las Vegas, New Mexico, and starred Edward James Olmos, airing on PBS; and *Wild Times*, perhaps New Mexico's first miniseries. *Cortez* was directed by Robert M. Young and is quite true to the actual events that revolve around the mistranslation of a few words of Spanish to English which leads to a shooting and a very long chase.

Several movies have nearly disappeared, such as *Second-Hand Hearts* (1981), which had the working title of *Hamster of Happiness* and starred Robert Blake. This picture was directed by a rising star in the business, Hal Ashby, who previously had directed a number of well-received titles such as *Coming Home* and *Bound for Glory*. His personal life interceded, and he tragically died of cancer in 1988. *Second-Hand Hearts* spent some time in the Orogrande area of southern New Mexico, just a short distance from the Mexican border.

There were also two productions sponsored by KGGM TV of Albuquerque, *1313 Broadcast Plaza* (aka *Amy*) and *Like Fine Wine*. No copies of these films are known to exist, and a phone conversation with Andrew Hebenstreit of the family who once owned (and founded) the station revealed that the productions didn't go well. With tongue in cheek, he said I should not ask him to go look for a copy of either picture.

The Comeback Trail (1982) also seems to have disappeared in spite of the fact that the great Buster Krabbe (*Tarzan*) was a co-star, this being his last film. Hugh Hefner, publisher of *Playboy* magazine, also had a small role.

Another 1980 release had so much controversy and bad press that it caused its first-time star, Klinton Spilsbury, to quit the industry entirely, much to the relief of many of those who worked with him on the set of *The Legend of the Lone Ranger*. Spilsbury was made into a rising star when cast as the lead for the film, which was partially shot around Santa Fe. Jason Robards signed on to play President Grant, and Christopher Lloyd took the role of Butch Cavendish, the chief bad guy. Michael Horse, a new actor who is a real American Indian, played Tonto, the famed second to the Ranger.

The producers of the film were determined to destroy the old image of the real Lone Ranger, who was played by Clayton Moore on the beloved television series. One of them even owned the rights to the show and forbade Moore from wearing the famous eye mask that he used at public appearances. He remained popular even though the television show had ended in 1957. To get around this odd ban, Moore wore wraparound sunglasses and maintained his claim to the character for many years after winning a counter lawsuit.

Spilsbury, on the other hand, didn't seem quite ready for the stardom that was thrust on him and asked for many concessions on the set, which were obliged, since he was the new image for an old franchise.

However, the whole production came undone over time, and the film was finally released six months after the original release date. It included a complete dubbing of Spilsbury's voice by actor/director James Keach since it was thought that Spilsbury's voice did not carry well, and instead of asking him to redo the scenes, they completely eliminated his voice.

It was Spilsbury's first and last film. At this writing, he remains unwilling to be interviewed about the experience, especially when another reworking of *The Lone Ranger* was released in 2013. That version of the Masked Man was also mostly shot in New Mexico.

The Day After Trinity, an interesting documentary, also gave New Mexico some exposure, using footage and interviews about J. Robert Oppenheimer, who was the head of the famed Manhattan Project that developed the atomic bomb in Los Alamos, New Mexico. The film was nominated for an Oscar for Best Documentary but was not chosen for the award.

Wrong Is Right, a satirical look at politics and American news reporting, also found itself giving New Mexico credit for shooting time. Starring Sean Connery, Katherine Ross and current Taos resident and artist Dean Stockwell, *Wrong Is Right* didn't win any awards, but it did have a great time lampooning many holy grails while filming around Albuquerque and Alamogordo, located in the south-central part of the state.

By mid-decade, things were again looking up for the state as a place to shoot. Bigger-budget productions came to the area, including the Meryl Streep picture *Silkwood* (1983), the previously discussed *Silverado* and the surprise hit *Red Dawn* (1984). Although only part of *Silkwood* was shot in New Mexico (Albuquerque and Los Alamos), it was an important film. It is based on the true-life story of Karen Silkwood, a whistleblower who challenged the energy giant Kerr-McGee concerning possible radiation leaks that were contaminating employees at an Oklahoma plant.

Silkwood herself was no angel, but her involvement became an awakening for her, and she later died under mysterious circumstances in an auto crash in 1974 while on her way to meet a reporter from the *New York Times*. After her death, an autopsy revealed plutonium contamination in her body.

With Streep in the lead role, the picture received fine support from co-stars Kurt Russell and Cher, with wonderful direction by Mike Nichols (*The Graduate*, 1967; *Catch-22*, 1970). Nichols made an extra effort to show Karen as a real person and not a martyr to her cause. She sometimes drank too much, dabbled in drugs and had an ongoing fight with an ex for custody of her children. Nichols managed to make her into a believable character.

The story eventually faded away until the mid-'90s, when it was revealed that the Los Alamos National Lab still had some of Karen's bone fragments and possibly her brain as well, which was removed during the autopsy without knowledge of her family.

Red Dawn, on the other hand—which was put onto film in and around Las Vegas and Abiquiu, New Mexico—takes a look at what might have been the start of World War III. Russian, Cuban and Nicaraguan paratroopers land in the small town of Calumet, Colorado, and are soon in charge of the area before being challenged by a group of guerrilla fighter high school students, with assistance from a couple of adults.

This movie was the film debut of Charlie Sheen, and director John Milius also directed *Conan the Barbarian* and wrote the screenplay for *Apocalypse Now*.

A true treasure of a film, *Lust in the Dust* was released in 1985 after shooting in and around Santa Fe, utilizing both movie ranches near the city, Eaves and Bonanza Creek. An always funny and cheesy comedy and a parody of *Duel in the Sun*, a noted 1946 western, this film stars Tab Hunter and Divine, aka Glenn Milstead, who frequently worked with John Waters (*Pink Flamingos*, 1972; *Hairspray*, 1988). It might be the first time that two genuine gay men played the lead actors in a western.

Divine plays a saloon girl on her way to Chile Verde, New Mexico, but before she gets there, she is found by Hunter's character, a true parody of Clint Eastwood's "Man with No Name," from his euro-westerns such as *A Fistful of Dollars*. Once in town, they need to contend with any number of greedy and goofy characters played by Lainie Kazan, Ned Romero, Geoffrey Lewis, Henry Silva and Woody Strode.

Road movies were big during the mid-'80s in New Mexico. Among them were the 1985 releases *Little Treasure*, with Margot Kidder, Ted Danson and Burt Lancaster; *Lost in America*, with Albert Brooks, which has a few brief scenes done in southern New Mexico; and *Fool for Love*, based on a play by Sam Shepard, a current part-time resident of Santa Fe, and directed by the great Robert Altman, who shot this picture just outside Santa Fe.

In 1986, *Blue De Ville* sped along the highways of northern New Mexico, with stops in Santa Fe, Las Vegas, Pecos and Glorieta. This made-for-TV film is a comedy about two women and a hitchhiker who are looking for the long-lost father of one of the women.

Outrageous Fortune (1987) continued the spate of road movies, with Bette Midler and Shelley Long traveling cross-county to find the man that they were both dating who has mysteriously disappeared. The movie also features the late, great comedian George Carlin as an American Indian, an odd role for the always acerbic and always Anglo Carlin. The film claims four New Mexico shooting sites: Santa Fe, Albuquerque, Abiquiu and Cerrillos. It was a box office winner, pulling in over $65 million for Touchstone Studios.

Inexplicably, director Roger Vadim came to Santa Fe to remake one of his own films, *And God Created Woman*, which was originally released in 1956 and starred Bridget Bardot. This 1988 release was shot in northern New Mexico, mostly around Santa Fe, and utilized the now-abandoned state prison, which has since been used in many other films. Rebecca De Mornay played the role that Bardot once filled after Madonna and Lisa Bonet were considered. Vadim's other obscure connection to New Mexico might be that he was once married to a Pecos, New Mexico resident, actress Jane Fonda.

Life on the road continued in 1987 when another small-budget road movie, *Made in USA*, was partially shot around Acoma Pueblo and in the northwest corner of the state near Farmington and Shiprock. Lori Singer is the only cast member of note.

It wasn't until the late '80s that filmmakers returned to New Mexico in great numbers. In 1988 alone, thirteen films that were made at least partially in the state were released, including two of the biggest of the year, *Young Guns I* and *Rain Man*.

There is a bit of a question about *Rain Man*, but if one watches closely and knows his geography, it seems that there are a couple of scenes shot in Tucumcari as the two brothers, played by Tom Cruise and Dustin Hoffman, head west. This film made more money than any other movie released in 1988 and also toted home four Academy Awards, including one for Best Picture, from the eight it was nominated for.

Young Guns I—codenamed *Young Buns* by a few wags since many of the actors in the film were young, handsome and popular at the time—became an interesting phenomenon that helped to briefly revive the western genre. The film was shot in several New Mexico locations, including the village of Cerrillos, just south of Santa Fe, and the small towns of Galisteo, Ojo Caliente and the Tesuque Pueblo. With a budget of $13 million and a cast that included the rising stars of Emilio Estevez as Billy the Kid and Kiefer Sutherland, Lou Diamond Phillips and Charlie Sheen as a few of his pals, the film took in almost $45 million and produced a sequel, *Young Guns II*, released in 1990. Many consider *Young Guns II* one of the few sequels that is better than the original. It is also considered one of the more historically accurate of the numerous movies that include Billy as a character or a subject. Just within New Mexico, at least seven feature films have included William Bonney, aka Billy the Kid, along with at least five documentaries. Oddly, the first film that featured the Kid was a short silent 1911 picture with actress Edith Storey playing Billy. This film was not made in New Mexico.

The other major picture released in 1988 that has a huge New Mexico connection is the ultra New Mexico–centric *The Milagro Beanfield War*. Based on a novel that is part of a trilogy by Taos, New Mexico author John Nichols, this film was shot mostly in the Truchas area of northern New Mexico, with other scenes shot near Santa Fe and Espanola. Robert Redford directed the film. It received some nasty comments due to the fact that some of the cast did not fit the roles of native New Mexicans since they were from other places. Sonia Braga is Brazilian, and Rubén Blades is from Panama. Nichols later wrote an essay about how torturous it was to get his book to the screen, "Night of the Living Beanfield: How an Unsuccessful Cult Novel Became an Unsuccessful Cult Film in Only Fourteen Years, Eleven Nervous Breakdowns, and $20 Million." Sadly, the picture lost about $10 million at the box office. Perhaps that is because it is so New Mexico "focused," meaning only residents or frequent visitors to the state would get a lot of the in-jokes concerning life in the "Land of Entrapment." Nonetheless, it is required viewing for all residents of the state.

The other films using New Mexico locations through 1988 were small pictures, although famed singer/songwriter Willie Nelson was on hand to shoot a picture around Santa Fe and Chama entitled *Where the Hell's that Gold*, a made-for-TV western comedy shot in just three weeks.

If you are into bad horror films, then 1988 was your year, since *The Brainsuckers* and *Curse II: The Bite* also lay claim to New Mexico film history. It is hard to decide which movie is worse.

The decade closed with seven productions from New Mexico being released in 1989, including one of the first films in years to use real First Nations actors in lead roles, *Powwow Highway*.

Based on a book by David Seals—currently a resident of Raton, New Mexico, and a member of the Huron Nation—the movie starred Gary Farmer as Philbert. Philbert, along with his friend Buddy Red Bow (A.

Martinez), both of whom have Native American roots, leaves his home in south-central Montana to go to Santa Fe to bail Red Bow's sister out of jail. It becomes a vision quest for the affable Philbert and a journey of discovery for Red Bow.

Directed by a native of South Africa, Jonathan Wacks, the film won him a Filmmakers Trophy at the esteemed Sundance Film Festival and a nomination for the Grand Jury Prize in 1989.

Several other smaller productions also took place, including *Time Out*, made by a Danish film company, and *High Desert Kill*, a horror film shot around the Santa Clara Pueblo, south of Santa Fe.

One of the biggest New Mexico–made productions of all time also was released that year, the epic western *Lonesome Dove*. Much of this seven-hour miniseries was shot in northern New Mexico. The series starred Robert Duvall, Tommy Lee Jones, Danny Glover and Diane Lane and won two Golden Globe Awards while being nominated for seventeen in total.

It is based on a Pulitzer Prize–winning book by author Larry McMurtry that tells the tale of two former Texas Rangers who decide to do a cattle drive to Montana. McMurtry originally wrote it as a script but was turned down many times, after which he decided to write the novel. The series also spawned several sequels and a prequel, *Comanche Moon*, which was also a New Mexico production. *Lonesome Dove* remains at the top of many film lovers' "Ten Best Westerns" lists.

Personal trivia: as a visitor in Santa Fe during the filming of the series, I happened upon Duvall on the Santa Fe Plaza, where we tipped hats to each other.

Although film crews kept coming to New Mexico on a regular basis in the '90s, when one looks at the roster of titles, it seems that each year produced one major film that did well at the box office and a number of others that either barely saw the light of day or withered on the vine.

In 1990, six films with a New Mexico connection were released, including *Sonny Boy*, an almost incomprehensible piece starring David Carradine and shot in far southern New Mexico; *Sparks: The Price of Passion*, a made-for-television opus about the trials and tribulations of a female mayor in a big southwestern city who also seems to spend most of her paycheck on clothes; and *Backtrack*, another oddity directed by and starring Taos resident Dennis Hopper, along with a young Jodie Foster, which has an unforgettable scene featuring a burrito. But the big hit that year was *Young Guns II*, which followed the success of the 1988 release of *Young Guns I*. Most of the surviving members of Billy the Kid's gang are along for the ride in this picture, which was shot largely in northern New Mexico, around Cerrillos, but also has a bit of footage from White Sands. It continues the fable of William Bonney and suggests that Bonney escaped and was never shot by Pat Garrett. Rather, the film opens with star Emilio Estevez portraying an old man who summons a lawyer to help him gain the amnesty promised to him many years before. This links to the real-life tale of "Brushy Bill" Roberts, who claimed to be the Kid until his death in 1950.

The film made $25 million at the box office, slightly less than the original *Young Guns I* made, which was about $31 million. It was a nice reward for director Geoff Murphy of New Zealand, who later returned to New Mexico to film the very violent post–Civil War western, *The Last Outlaw*, which aired in 1993 on HBO.

As the decade progressed, filmmakers still had adoration for New Mexico, with about ten productions a year ending up in the state. As a result, there were many smaller films, but each year seemed to crank out one film that received a big release and made some money.

In 1991, of the ten films that the state receives some credit for, several—such as *Adobe Angels*, directed by Bob Chinn—aren't available for viewing nor are any synopses available. A quick search finds that the *Adobe Angels* was apparently shot in Albuquerque, but no details are available.

But the big title for 1991 was *City Slickers*, which not only is one of the funniest movies ever shot partially in New Mexico but is also one of the few that allowed a cast member, Jack Palance in this instance, to take home an Oscar. Palance won the award for his portrayal of Curly, who heads up a bunch of city slickers on a cattle drive hosted by a guest ranch. The film also stars Billy Crystal and Daniel Stern, who also was a co-star in *The Milagro Beanfield War*. The picture was shot in Abiquiu, the Nambe and Santa Clara Pueblos and Santa Fe. Although the film cost $27 million to make, it has brought back handsome returns, including $60 million just in video rentals as of 2015.

The science fiction drama-comedy *Late for Dinner* was also released in 1991. This odd little film finds two young men, charged with a crime they didn't commit, being cryogenically frozen in the '60s and revived in the '90s. It was shot at many different locations in the state, including Santa Fe and several other towns in northern New Mexico. It was also the film debut of comedienne/actress Janeane Garofalo.

Lucky Luke came to town as well. This film led to a four-part television series, with each episode being two hours in length. It never played in the United States, only in Europe, and was based on a comic book of the same name created by Belgian artist Maurice De Bevere. *Lucky Luke* also spawned several video games, a 2009 Argentinean feature film and a number of animated series.

The New Mexico version starred and was directed by Terrence Hill (aka Mario Girotti), whose name became very prominent back in the days of euro-westerns (westerns shot mostly in Spain by Italian crews in the '60s and often featuring an American lead actor supported by Spanish and Italian casts).

Hill, who now lives in Massachusetts, has been in New Mexico numerous times to shoot other films, including part of *My Name Is Nobody* (1972), a comic western with Henry Fonda. That movie was shot partially in Mogollan, New Mexico, in the far western part of the state, and also at White Sands and the San Ilfdenso Pueblo.

Doc West and *Triggerman*, both comedy westerns that were shot at Santa Fe's Bonanza Creek Movie Ranch in 2009, were also part of Hill's repertoire. Hill also made *The Night Before Christmas* (aka *Troublemakers)* at Bonanza Creek.

Another odd little comedy was shot in the Las Cruces area, the first film that had been shot in that area for almost fifteen years. *Vaya Con Dios* (aka *Hard Time Romance*) was director John Lee Hancock's film debut. Hancock has since gone on to bigger projects, including *The Blind Side*, which won an Oscar for Sandra Bullock; *Saving Mr. Banks*; and the remake of *The Alamo*. None of these was shot in New Mexico, but Hancock's auspicious start did begin with a small romantic comedy shot in the deserts of southern New Mexico.

The year 1992 finally saw a woman director in New Mexico, when Allison Anders came to the small town of Deming, New Mexico, for her coming-of-age film *Gas, Food, Lodging*. The picture is also unique for New Mexico–made movies since women (Ione Skye, Brooke Adams and Fairuza Balk) play the three leads. The crew was also made up mostly of women and was screened at a number of large film festivals, including Sundance, Montreal and Berlin.

An interesting small film shot in the Santa Fe area was *God Drives a Pontiac*, directed by Rex "Hoss" Thompson. The plot involves a down-on-his-luck car salesman who runs the Church of the Used Car, which attracts any number of oddball characters, including Snakegirl and Elvis. Thompson's budget was miniscule, but the results of this hard-to-find film are worth their weight in gold.

The other big film of the year was *White Sands*, which features Willem Dafoe, Samuel L. Jackson, Mary Elizabeth Mastrantonio and Mickey Rourke. It is an exciting murder mystery directed by Australian Roger Donaldson and was filmed mostly around Estancia in central New Mexico, but also at Taos Gorge and in Santa Fe. Kevin Costner, Jeff Bridges and

Nick Nolte were considered for lead roles, but the budget wouldn't allow for them to be signed. Both Bridges and Costner have made New Mexico movies, while Nolte still awaits his big-screen break in the state.

The award for best missing film of 1992 would have to go to *La Llorona*, of which the only information available notes shooting locations (Cochiti Pueblo, Galisteo and Santa Fe); director Marc Miles; and star Jill Scott Momaday, daughter of Pulitzer Prize–winning author N. Scott Momaday, whose writing produced 1987's *House Made of Dawn*, a small-budget picture shot in New Mexico.

Releases in 1993 were again numerous, but again, they were all small-budget works—except one, of course: *Speechless*, which stars Geena Davis and Michael Keaton. Shot in Las Vegas, Albuquerque, Los Alamos, Santa Fe and the village of San Jose, the film is a romantic comedy that has Davis and Keaton as speechwriters working for opposing candidates in the New Mexico gubernatorial election. It was directed by Ron Underwood, who must have liked what he saw when he came to New Mexico earlier to film *City Slickers*. Since 2005, Underwood has only done work on television shows and made-for-television movies, but he made a nice impression in New Mexico with these two fun comedy pictures.

Another film of note is *Paper Hearts*, also known as *Cheatin' Hearts*, which was shot entirely on location by a director who actually lives in New Mexico. Rod McCall lives part time in the village of Hillsboro in southwestern New Mexico and also in Las Cruces during the school year, as he is an instructor at New Mexico State University's Creative Media Institute.

Paper Hearts stars Sally Kirkland and James Brolin in a drama about a man who returns to his family after deserting them and leaving them in dire financial straits. This film premiered at the Sundance Film Festival, as did McCall's dark comedy *Lewis and Clark and George*, which was also shot in New Mexico. McCall did some filming for that work in the towns of Kingston and Truth or Consequences, New Mexico. He continues to shoot only in his adopted home state. His newest project, *Jim*, was shot in the Las Cruces area and is making the festival circuit in 2015.

Most of the other '93 releases have little to talk about, although *Road Scholar*, a documentary about a road trip across the United States with stops in Santa Fe and Taos, New Mexico, by National Public Radio journalist and newly licensed driver Andrei Codrescu is a humorous look at life in America.

Once again, there was a lost film, *Rio Shannon*, directed by Mimi Leder. The film stars Blair Brown and offers the experiences of a recently widowed woman and her family who move to New Mexico for a new start on an old ranch that they try to turn into a posh hotel. The movie, which was a pilot for a potential series, played on ABC and was shot in the Galisteo area, in Santa Fe and also around Abiquiu and the Tesuque Pueblo and then promptly disappeared.

Additionally, there were three other made-for-television productions that made their small-screen debut in 1993, including *New Eden*, *The Fire Next Time* and *The Last Hit*.

Famed playwright Sam Shepard also returned to his old home state to shoot an unusual western with River Phoenix and Richard Harris, *Silent Tongue*. This picture was one of the few features ever shot on the eastern plains of New Mexico, near the city of Roswell. It also tanked at the box office, making only $61,000, but it was also only shown in three theaters.

Oddly, Phoenix, who died just a few months before the film was released, made two of his last three movies in New Mexico. The other, *Dark Blood*, was given a limited release almost twenty years after it was shot, in an altered form, with director George Sluizer filling in the gaps left by Phoenix's passing with narration and stills since it was never really finished. That picture was partially shot in the Gallup area.

In 1994 and '95, productions shot in New Mexico continued to be released on a very regular basis. Made-for-television and cable productions lead the way, with seven creations done for that media. The lost films for these two years include *Greenhorn*, a German television production shot around Farmington, Las Vegas and Albuquerque; *Cultivating Charlie*; and another made-for-television piece, *Doc Holliday: The Man and the Legend*. The filming of this work took place in Shakespeare, New Mexico, a ghost town in the far southwest corner of the state in July 1993. However, there is not much other information about it, except that it was written and produced by Colleen D. Dawson and starred Erich Hauser, a relative of Wings Hauser, a fairly well-known actor during that period.

A photo of Erich Hauser on his imdb.com page has him in cowboy regalia, but the film is not listed on his filmography. The film was completed, which was verified by a gentleman who answered the phone at Shakespeare where tours of the town's remains are offered several times a year.

"I did see it," he commented, "but I never heard of it again after they showed it here," he said and hung up. Perhaps he was a ghost.

Cultivating Charlie has a different and sad story. Upon completion of the film, which had a $2 million budget and a cast that included the noted Dr. Timothy Leary of LSD fame, one of the two thirty-five-millimeter prints was stolen from the trunk of a rental car being used by the producers. The thieves made off with seventy pounds of film and reels. The only other print made it to the South by Southwest Film Festival in Austin, Texas, and the Dallas Film Festival, but beyond that, not much is known about this picture, which was partially shot in four New Mexico locations: Espanola, Albuquerque, Las Vegas and Santa Fe.

After the theft, *Variety Magazine* quoted Raquel Haber, a co-producer of the film, "It was ironic that it was stolen in Hollywood of all places. What are you going to do with all that film? It's just so frustrating." The film was said to be a comic and updated version of Voltaire's *Candide*.

Two of the most violent films ever shot in these here parts were also screened in 1994: *The Last Outlaw*, a made-for-cable western with Mickey Rourke and Dermot Mulroney, and *Natural Born Killers*, directed by Oliver Stone and starring Woody Harrelson and Juliette Lewis.

The latter film is part crime story, part romance and part satire. It hooks onto the glorification and media coverage given to serial killers. Lewis and

Woody Harrelson and Juliette Lewis starred in *Natural Born Killers*, which attempted to show how the media often portrays wrong as right. *Courtesy of John Armijo.*

Harrelson are Mallory and Mickey, who create carnage and death wherever they stop but always seem to leave one survivor so that person can report to the media what they have seen. The movie received a lot of press coverage due to the content, which temporarily raised awareness about how criminals are usually overvalued while their victims are often forgotten.

The film was shot partially at the beautiful Rio Grande Gorge near Taos, Albuquerque, San Jose, Las Vegas, Shiprock, Gallup and Farmington. It did well at the box office in spite of the controversy surrounding the body count.

The Last Outlaw, filmed around Santa Fe, is a true anti-hero movie, and by the end, there is only one man standing.

Westerns dominated those two years, with the only national releases shot in New Mexico coming in 1994—*Wyatt Earp* and *The Cowboy Way*. Woody Harrelson returned to New Mexico to shoot the latter film, a comedy, starring with Keifer Sutherland as two modern-day cowpunchers who head to New York to help the daughter of a friend. Mischief ensues.

Wyatt Earp, on the other hand, while a fine film in its own right, fell victim to the other film featuring Earp as a character, *Tombstone*. *Tombstone* was released at the very end of 1993 and featured a stellar cast, with Kurt Russell starring as Earp, Val Kilmer as a very cynical Doc Holliday and Sam Elliott as Virgil Earp. The film did very well at the box office and added the phrase "I'm your huckleberry" to the lexicon of western fans worldwide—a phrase used several times by Kilmer while taunting gun-fighting opponents. Supposedly, the correct phrase is "I'm your huckle bearer," a term used for those who carry the deceased's casket. Huckles are the handles on a casket.

Wyatt Earp, on the other hand, might have had a better chance if it had been released as planned as a ten-part miniseries. Although it has a strong lead cast, with Kevin Costner as Earp and Dennis Quaid as Holliday, it lacked the cohesion that *Tombstone* displayed. While *Tombstone* made millions, *Wyatt Earp*, which was written and directed by Lawrence Kasdan—who also had done the very successful New Mexico feature *Silverado* about ten years earlier—lost millions. Kasdan's written oeuvre also includes *Raiders of the Lost Ark* (1980).

Tombstone was not shot in New Mexico, while *Wyatt Earp* could be found shooting in numerous places in and around Santa Fe and also in Chama.

A television miniseries that did do well was another western, *Buffalo Girls*. Starring Anjelica Huston as Calamity Jane Canary and Melanie Griffith as Dora DuFran, the series has Calamity Jane looking for her long-lost daughter in the Old West and encountering every "name" person of the times along the way, including Sitting Bull, the famous Hunkpapa Lakota war chief; George Armstrong Custer; Wild Bill Hickok; and, of course, Buffalo Bill

Cody. It won seven Primetime Emmy Awards and was nominated for two Golden Globes. It was shot in several locations around Santa Fe and Las Vegas, New Mexico.

Certainly one of the more unique and unusual westerns ever shot here is the 1995 Japanese film *East Meets West*. It is a lighthearted film featuring samurai warriors going from San Francisco to points east to protect a cache of gold. Most of the film was shot, again, in northern New Mexico, while paying its respects to several famous United States–produced westerns, including *The Cowboys* and *Shane*.

The years between 1996 and 1999 proved to be a fairly slow time for the film industry in New Mexico. There were over thirty productions, but most of these were made for cable or television or only used the state for a short time before moving on to another location. *Independence Day* was certainly the biggest title, but most of its New Mexico–related shots were cut.

In 1996, *Ravenhawk*, a tale of a female American Indian vigilante, featured a non-Native actress starring in the role. Rachel McLish, a former bodybuilding champ, plays the lead in this TV movie that did some shooting around Santa Fe.

Other movies made for cable markets abounded through the end of the '90s, including the heralded *The Lazarus Man* (1996), *Last Stand at Saber River* (1996), two episodes of *Walker, Texas Ranger* (1997) and *Scattering Dad* (1997). They were all prepared partially around Santa Fe, along with *Mary Jane Colter: House Made of Dawn*, a 1998 television special about the woman who designed many of the buildings for the famed Fred Harvey Company. Copies of this documentary are difficult to obtain, so it is not known at this time what area of New Mexico the film uses.

Films with small or short general releases in 1996 included *Infinity*, made partially in Las Vegas and Los Alamos, and *Last Man Standing*, made in Galisteo.

The romantic comedy *Fools Rush In*, released in 1997, was briefly in New Mexico and used Santa Fe's Rancho de los Golondrinas in a few scenes. Andrew Shea directed the very satirical comedy *Santa Fe*, which was shot entirely in New Mexico, mostly in Santa Fe. Shea, who was once a resident of the city, also founded the New Mexico Repertory Theatre, which remains one of the biggest and most successful stage production companies in the state. The film was co-written by Mark Medoff, also a successful playwright who lives in Las Cruces and teaches at the Creative Media Institute at New Mexico State University.

The Lazarus Man, a well-received television series about an amnesiac Civil War veteran, starred Robert Ulrich but only ran for one season. *Courtesy of John Armijo.*

Contact (1997), the Jodie Foster vehicle that shared part of central New Mexico with the world, made over $100 million at the box office and was certainly one of the most victorious films of the decade in terms of money and critical acclaim. But it was also beset with legal issues after filmmaker Francis Ford Coppola sued, claiming that he had proposed the same idea for a television series in 1975 to Carl Sagan, the co-producer of the film and the writer of the book that it is based on, asking Sagan to develop a script, which never occurred. Sagan's book came to print in 1985, and ten years later, the deal was made between Sagan and Warner Brothers studio to make the film.

Sagan passed away in late 1996 before the film was released, and it took until the year 2000 for a California Court of Appeals to dismiss the case, wherein Coppola asked for a share of the profit from both the book and movie. The court ruled that his claims "were brought too late."

As far as the movie goes, it doesn't seem too likely that there would be much money left, since it is said that Foster received a salary of $7 million for her work in the picture.

In the April 14, 2000 issue of *Daily Variety*, Coppola is quoted as saying, "I want your readers to know the falseness of the Carl Sagan lawyer's statement that I sued him 'six days after Sagan died.'" No matter. The film is a good one about the attempts at finding intelligent life in other galaxies, since so little of that exists on Earth.

The year 1997 has its own lost films. The oddest might be the Italian production *Lovest*, which found the filmmakers doing guerrilla-style shooting at White Sands National Monument. Certainly not the first crew to shoot without permits or permission on government property, it might be one of the few instances where the film was actually released in Europe but not in the United States.

It is said to be a road trip comedy with two friends traveling across the United States. It is directed by Guilio Base, who returned to New Mexico in 2008 for a small part in the western *Triggerman*.

The other sort of missing film is *The Trailblazer*, which was shot around Albuquerque and the Jemez Pueblo. Alexandra Pratt, the director, said in an e-mail, "The picture was never completely finished, so it was never released."

Following the pattern of the last twenty years, 1998 and 1999 each had one huge studio release, with *Armageddon* filling that niche in '98 and *Wild Wild West* in '99, each of which had budgets around $150 million. There also were some medium-budget pictures, such as *Vampires* (1998, $20 million), *Lolita* (1998, $50 million) and *The Bachelor* (1999, $21 million), and a variety of small-budget movies including *Soundman*, *The Outfitters* and the very successful and fun *The Tao of Steve*.

Wild Wild West, based on the terrific and innovative TV series of the '60s, was a disaster in almost every possible way. Not terribly entertaining even with big-name stars like Will Smith, Kenneth Branagh, Salma Hayek and Kevin Kline, the picture lost a ton of money. Later, Will Smith confessed that turning down a major role in *Matrix* for this unsettled western comedy was the "biggest mistake of his career." It was shot partially around Chama and Santa Fe, New Mexico.

Armageddon, which stars Bruce Willis, Ben Affleck and Billy Bob Thornton, did better at the box office but not so well critically. It uses New Mexico for a few brief scenes, mostly around Socorro in the central part of the state.

Lolita, a remake of the successful '60s film with James Mason, has a few brief second unit scenes in southern New Mexico in the Las Cruces area.

A remake of a fantastic Buster Keaton film, *The Bachelor* starred Renée Zellweger and Chris O'Donnell in a romantic comedy about a single guy who needs to marry in twenty-four hours in order to claim a huge inheritance. This adventure includes a road trip that uses the Cook Ranch in Galisteo for a few shots.

Vampires was directed by horror movie master John Carpenter. The filmmakers opted for the Santa Fe/Las Vegas area for their shoot. This bloody film features James Woods as a vampire hunter, with Sheryl Lee and Daniel Baldwin as co-stars.

Albuquerque and Santa Fe were the settings for *Soundman*, a romantic comedy about a guy who works as a sound mixer for movies who tries to get a woman he is in love with some work scoring films even though she is a talentless violinist.

The Outfitters was shot in central New Mexico, around the mountain town of Ruidoso and is a comedy about two brothers trying to drum up cash to save their father's run-down ranch.

But the best of this bunch has to be *The Tao of Steve*, which is based on the true story of a friend/roommate of director Jenniphr Goodman. Her friend is a slouchy, overweight elementary school teacher who, in spite of his lackadaisical attitude, has great success at getting women into bed.

The feature won the star Donal Logue a Special Jury Prize for Outstanding Performance in a Narrative Film at the Sundance Film Festival, and the picture itself was nominated for the festival's Grand Jury Prize but did not win.

Made-for-TV movies during these two years included *The Staircase*, with Barbara Hershey, which tells the story of the mythical, miracle staircase at the Chapel of Loretto in Santa Fe (where the film was shot), and *Wishbone: Dog Days of the West* (1998), a little comedy based on the popular PBS character who is now in the Old West helping to keep the bad guys at bay. This movie was filmed at the Cook and Eaves Movie Ranches. There is also *Gunfighters of the West* (1999), a television series shot around northern New Mexico, and *On the Beam: Learning at the Creative Edge of Risk* (1999), a documentary for PBS.

Another almost forgotten film, *Palmer's Pickup* (1999), did some second unit shooting in far southwestern New Mexico. The indie film *Jesus Freak*, which

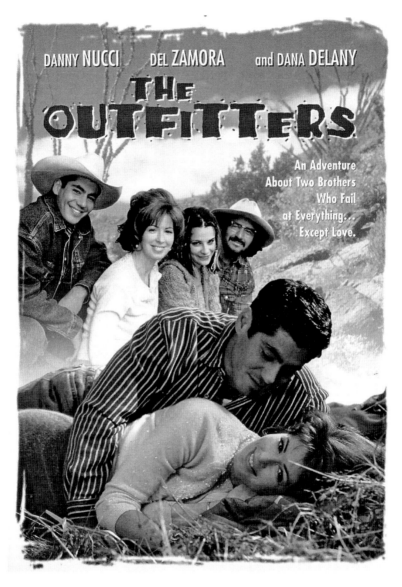

The 1999 release *The Outfitters*, a comedy adventure film, is one of the few to be shot in the beautiful mountain town of Ruidoso, New Mexico. *From the collection of John Armijo.*

may have actually been released in 2003 rather than 1999, became the first film ever shot in Portales, New Mexico, in the far eastside of the state.

Although several of these films have their own good stories, the one that has the most impact is *The Hi-Lo Country* (1998). Based on the book of the

BARBARA HERSHEY   WILLIAM PETERSEN

Between a woman's courage

and a stranger's kindness,

a miracle occurred.

the Staircase

A Craig Anderson Production in association with BWE Distribution, Inc. and Television
Produced by Marty Schwartz. Executive Producers Craig Anderson and Jeffrey F. Grant. Co-Produced /Written by Christopher Lofton. Directed by Karen Arthur

The ponderous *The Staircase*, a made-for-television movie screened in 1998, helped reinforce the myth of the "mysterious" staircase in Santa Fe's famed Loretto Chapel. *Courtesy of John Armijo.*

same name by classic New Mexican author Max Evans, the story is based on his experiences as a cowboy during the post–World War II era. The film stars Woody Harrelson, Billy Crudup, Patricia Arquette, Penelope Cruz and Sam Elliott and was directed by Stephen Frears.

At its peak, this beautiful western had a release to a total of sixteen theaters, according to Box Office Mojo. Even though it was released by Gramercy/Polygram Pictures, which had been a pretty big player at the time, the company soon went under and the film went with it. "Polygram was the production company, and it was taken over by Universal [Studios] while we were filming," Evans recalled. "They had two pictures and just enough money to promote and release one—*Elizabeth*, which earned Cate Blanchett an Oscar. They just threw *The Hi-Lo Country* away."

Frears—who is from Great Britain and whose résumé includes such films as *Dangerous Liaisons* (1998) and *The Queen* (2006)—decided to do the film in part because he's "always wanted to direct a western," as he shared at the Santa Fe Film Festival.

Evans was a friend of the late director Sam Peckinpah (*The Wild Bunch*, *Pat Garrett and Billy the Kid*), and Peckinpah worked for years to try to get the film made, optioning it in 1961 and then attempting to produce it in 1973. But the script was never quite right, nor could he get the OK from a studio to make the film. Eventually and slightly ironically, Walon Green, who did the script for Peckinpah's masterpiece *The Wild Bunch*, did the same for *Hi-Lo*.

Frears won a Best Director prize at the 1999 Berlin Film Festival, while the picture won the Western Heritage Wrangler Award from the National Cowboy Hall of Fame that same year for the "Best Film About the West." Additionally, in 2002, *Book* magazine selected the movie as one of the "100 Best Film Adaptations of All Time."

Evans first worked for Peckinpah when he had a small but fun part in the comic western *The Ballad of Cable Hogue*, and they became lifelong friends. In 2014, *Goin' Crazy with Sam Peckinpah* was released, which was a memoir as told to journalist Robert Nott about Evans's time with Peckinpah. Evans also published a slim volume, *Sam Peckinpah: Master of Violence*, in 1972.

In an article by Nott in the *Santa Fe New Mexican* on May 17, 2013, Evans said that Peckinpah, trying to obtain the rights to *Hi-Lo*, told Evans's agent, "I want to meet the son of a bitch who wrote it." In the article, Nott wrote:

> *Evans and his wife, Pat, were attending the Cowboy Hall of Fame awards ceremony in Oklahoma City in the mid-1990s when one of their daughters called them from Albuquerque to tell them that Martin Scorsese had left a phone message for Max. Actor L.Q. Jones, a friend of Evans' and frequent actor for Peckinpah, had just worked for Scorsese in* Casino *and suggested that Scorsese read* The Hi-Lo Country *and adapt it for film. Scorsese wrote Evans a letter asking about the rights and expressing admiration for the book. "He said he understood why Sam [Peckinpah] wanted to make the picture—because of the characters." Evans said.*

The movie was shot mostly on location all over northern and northeast New Mexico, where a lot of the real story that Evans relates actually took place. It flopped at the box office, making only about $170,000 during its brief release. Evans once told me that he had been told that only one thirty-five-millimeter print of the film was saved for reasons he was not sure of.

Released almost immediately on VHS, the DVD version was nearly impossible to find after a very short run, until 2012, when it was re-released by Shout! Factory.

7

GIVE ME A BREAK AND WE'LL FILM IN NEW MEXICO

Until now, my research has netted little in the way of reasons why studios and directors and others took to New Mexico over the years, other than the efforts by Governor David Cargo, author Max Evans and a host of others back around 1970 to sell New Mexico. And sell it they did! I've offered bits and pieces and trivia for many of the films covered thus far since little information is readily available for them.

This section will focus on a few films made during the first dozen years that the tax incentive program was in effect.

It didn't take long for the film industry to take advantage of the incentives package after then governor Gary Johnson signed off on a bill in 2002 that would soon open many doors for moviemakers of all varieties. There has been a huge increase in film and television productions in New Mexico because of the film incentive program that began in earnest in 2003 and continues as I write this volume.

Since the start of the incentive program in 2003 and through mid-2015, by my count, 392 film and television productions have come to New Mexico to take advantage of the program. In 2012, there were at least forty-three crews in the state shooting a film or show that was at least one hour in length, which can also mean an episode of a series, such as *Breaking Bad*. The year 2008 came up one short, with forty-two films or television episodes being at least shot in part in this state.

Prior to 2003, about 420 movies and such were made in New Mexico, including the 50-plus short films made between 1897 and 1916. That is a total of over 800 productions from 1897 through mid-2015. If one were to look on IMDB.com and do a search for "New Mexico," a list of over 2,000 titles comes up, but they are also broken down into individual television episodes, some short films and others that are suspect in terms of whether any or all of a particular show was shot in New Mexico.

The two years leading up to the start of the incentive program pretty much kept the same pace and variety as earlier years. In 2000 and 2001, there were sixteen productions of one sort or another in New Mexico, with a number of small-budget films being done along with two major releases, both in 2000, *Traffic* and *All the Pretty Horses*.

Traffic in particular was a huge film that year. Only a very tiny part of the film was located in New Mexico, that being at the Las Cruces airport. The film won four Oscars, and the box office earnings tripled the budget.

All the Pretty Horses was directed by Billy Bob Thornton, and sadly, the picture lost millions of dollars in spite of a great cast and interesting story. Reviewers roundly criticized it. Much of the film was shot, once again, in northern New Mexico, within a day of Santa Fe or Taos.

Oddly, it was nominated for a number of awards worldwide but just did not catch on with audiences. Supposedly, the director's cut of the film was three hours and forty minutes long. The released version checks in at just under than two hours, which might explain the lack of continuity in the released version.

Another film by a "known" director was released in 2001, *John Carpenter's Ghosts of Mars*, which was filmed around the Zia Pueblo and the Albuquerque vicinity, mostly in an old gypsum mine that had to be spray painted red in order to look like Mars. This movie lost millions at the box office as well.

Most of the New Mexico–made films put out in 2002 were limited releases, including a couple of excellent documentaries, *Rocks with Wings*, *Trail of the Painted Ponies* and *The Silence of Cricket Coogler*. In fact, all of the films that were released that year were documentaries except one.

Collecting Rooftops is a comedy shot around Albuquerque but probably was never released. Another film, *The Rovers*, which seems to be unavailable for viewing, might be a documentary based on a theater production group based in Taos. Its content remains a mystery at this time.

Things really started to roll in 2003 and 2004. Just fewer than thirty releases came from New Mexico over those two years, including smaller works such as *Chooch*, a clever comedy shot along the New Mexico/

Mexico border, and *Warrior Women-Lozen*, a biographical piece about a woman warrior of the Apache Nation.

Television seems to have really discovered the incentive program, with the History Channel releasing a show about Kit Carson and Buffalo Bill and another on Billy the Kid. A number of documentaries filmed in New Mexico, such as *Santa Fe Mainline*, about the Atchison, Topeka and Santa Fe rail line, also came out in 1998, to the delight of train enthusiasts.

But things were on the upswing. A lot of work came from major studios, including the underrated western *The Missing*, with Ron Howard in the director's chair and Tommy Lee Jones heading a stellar cast that included Cate Blanchett.

Coyote Waits and *A Thief of Time*, based on New Mexican writer Tony Hillerman's Leaphorn and Chee novels, were shot in the state for PBS and directed by Chris Eyre, whose debut film, *Smoke Signals*, has become a mainstay of American Indian cinema.

21 Grams, a huge hit, starred Sean Penn and Naomi Watts and was probably one of the films that really got other filmmakers to notice the incentive program. Filmed in and around Albuquerque and the Zia Pueblo, it also led to another big film, the biggest one ever principally shot beyond in southern New Mexico. In 2009, *The Burning Plain* came to screens, and even though it didn't do well with ticket sales, it brought a much-needed boost to the film community of Las Cruces, which is the second-largest city in the state. Director Guillermo Arriaga had been on the crew of *21 Grams* as the writer and was so impressed with Las Cruces that he insisted that the film office's location scout take him to that part of the state while he was looking for shooting locations. The film stars Charlize Theron and Jennifer Lawrence in one of her first feature films.

And the lost films for these years? Yes, there are a few, including *Cross* (2004), about which director Chris L. Dillon wrote, "This Film was produced with no budget and in the insane time frame of two months."

Wild Bill, which may have been also titled *Mean as Hell*, was also shot at the Bonanza Creek Ranch. The film seems, at least for now, to be lost in the void. *Around the Bend* is a great road movie about four generations of the same family on a road trip to New Mexico, all of them discovering themselves and each other. Christopher Walken helps make this film a "must see."

The boom continued during the next two years, when over fifty films with a link to New Mexico were released, and the number of high-quality projects was also on the rise. The winner of the Oscar for Best Picture for 2005, *Brokeback Mountain*, had a very brief scene shot in Mesilla, New

Mexico. *Wildfire*, an ABC television series, landed in New Mexico and ran for four seasons. *Glory Road* helped give a bit of exposure to southern New Mexico, too. And although the budgets for many of these films were small, the word of mouth generated by these productions certainly helped attract high rollers to the state.

It might be that a producer or agent who endured 2006's *Beerfest* (a movie where New Mexico stars as Munich, Germany) told someone, who told someone else, who later told Joel and Ethan Coen to come to New Mexico to make outstanding pictures such as the remake of *True Grit* or *No Country for Old Men*.

Two films of particular interest emerged between 2005 and 2007. One is *The Flock* (2007), which became a political hot potato in the 2010 New Mexico gubernatorial election. With the tax incentive program firmly in place and filmmakers running to New Mexico, an incident occurred during the making of that movie that was brought to the attention of then candidate, now governor Susana Martinez.

Richard Gere was the star of the film, which cost $35 million to make and apparently was never released in the United States, thus losing millions at the box office. During the shoot for this film, Gere's private jet was chartered to take him elsewhere for a while at the expense of $100,000. And with the financial breaks being given, a bit of outrage ensued when it was noted that New Mexico taxpayers paid for 25 percent of that tab, $25,000, since it became a tax credit via the incentive program.

This incident became part of Martinez's platform to eliminate the incentives. Although she was elected, has since been reelected and was able to cut the plan for a while, it has since been revised and, in some cases, increased. What wasn't said any time during the campaign was that the loophole that allowed for Gere's travel (and possibly others as well) was closed and that the filmmakers even reimbursed the state for the funds that Martinez and others felt were misapplied.

It is fairly well known that a lot of people in Europe—especially in Germany and, to a lesser degree, in France—have a huge interest in the history of the Old West. Germany has weekend camps where people can role play as "American" Indians or other figures of that era, and some years ago, a handful of western films came from Germany, even some from what was then East Germany, all of which had Native Americans as heroes and good guys, defeating the hapless U.S. government.

In *Requiem for Billy the Kid*, French filmmaker Anne Feinsilber takes the story and myth of William Bonney to new heights by reexamining his time

A film that was unexpectedly a hit comedy, *Wild Hogs* helped stimulate the economy of the tiny artist colony of Madrid, New Mexico. *Courtesy of the New Mexico Film Office.*

and New Mexico via poetry, clips from other films and interviews with people who knew or were related to people who said they knew the Kid. Feinsilber also had the sheriff of Lincoln County, New Mexico, where Billy spent a lot of time, read some poetry, some of it by noted French poet Arthur Rimbaud, who is sometimes seen as a founder of French symbolism. It all ties in quite well but does make for a very esoteric movie.

The movie version of the hit Broadway play *Rent* (2005) has a couple scenes near the end of the film that were shot in Albuquerque, making it one of the first musicals to visit the state since the 1950s.

Wild Hogs, a midlife crisis comedy, was an unexpected hit when released in 2006. The film stars John Travolta, William H. Macy, Martin Lawrence and Tim Allen as four middle-aged family men who leave Cincinnati on a motorcycle trip west. Parts of the film were shot in the small town of Madrid, Santa Fe and Albuquerque.

No Country for Old Men (2007)—which won the Oscar for Best Picture that year, along with three other Academy Awards—was the first film to bring master filmmakers Joel and Ethan Coen to New Mexico. Filmed in Albuquerque, Santa Fe, Arroyo Hondo and Las Vegas, the movie was a huge box office hit. The Coens, as writers and directors, returned

Taos, a 2008 release, is proof positive that micro-budget movies are sometimes very well made and visceral. *Courtesy of the New Mexico Film Office.*

to shoot their magnificent remake of *True Grit* in 2010 in northern New Mexico.

One of the lead roles for *True Grit*, that of young Mattie Ross, went to first-time actress Hailee Steinfeld, who was chosen from fifteen thousand young women who applied for the part. Steinfeld was nominated for an Oscar, one of ten that the film received nominations for, but neither she nor the movie won an award.

The Coens also wrote the screenplay for the 2012 remake of *Gambit*, which saw some film work being done in Albuquerque and rural Bingham, New Mexico.

Another interesting western, *Seraphim Falls* (2007), used some of the beautiful desert areas around Lordsburg for shooting. The film stars Liam Neeson and Pierce Brosnan as rivals in this slightly ghostly revenge picture. American Indian actor Wes Studi has a bit part, and it is a bit embarrassing to note that when the credits run at the end of the film, they misspell his name twice (Studie) and Lordsburg has become Lodsburg.

For some years, those making feature films, rather than television work, picked up most of the incentive packages. The features had budgets and casts of all sizes, with titles such as *Klown Kamp Massacre* (2008); *Coyote County Loser* (2009), which was one of the first films shot in the Roswell area after incentives; and *Dead Man's Burden* (2011).

Crazy Heart, a feature film that wasn't expected to do much, ended up doing a lot when released in 2009. Not only did it feature a performance by Jeff Bridges that won him an Oscar, but it also won an Oscar for Best Original Song, which was co-written by Ryan Bingham, a native of Hobbs, New Mexico. Again shooting in the Santa Fe/Albuquerque area, it is the first feature film to include a scene shot at the beautiful Santa Fe Opera.

Comic books have also come to the silver screen via New Mexico in recent years, including parts of *Superman* (1978), *Iron Man II* (2010), *Thor* (2011) and *The Avengers* (2012), all doing some moviemaking in the Santa Fe and Albuquerque area. Perhaps the biggest of these comic book–based movies is scheduled for a 2016 release, *Batman v Superman: Dawn of Justice*, which somehow found the town of Deming in southwest New Mexico to use for part of the filming.

So what lies ahead for New Mexico movies? Will the film incentive packages continue to draw as they have been? Will the continued success of cable series such as *Longmire* and *Manhattan* and the past success and continued buzz for *Breaking Bad* remain topics of conversation? Will huge studio productions such as *Sicario* (2015), the poorly received revival of *The*

Lone Ranger (2013) and *Let Me In* (2010) be the standard bill of fare? Or will local businesses and state coffers need to rely on smaller flicks, like *Jim* (2015), *Bless Me Ultima* (2013) and *Beyond the Reach* (2015)? Besides loving films as works of art, I like to think of the popular bumper sticker one sees around the state when I think of New Mexico–made movie productions: "Movies Make Money for New Mexico."

8

PEOPLE AND PLACES

As it is noted throughout this book, almost every corner of New Mexico has seen some sort of filming activity over the years, and New Mexico itself has "starred" as numerous places as well. Albuquerque leads the way, with over one hundred shoots having taken place in or around the Duke City since the early 1900s. This figure has increased dramatically since the hugely successful *Breaking Bad* series.

Santa Fe is a close second, maybe by this time even with Albuquerque, due to its landscape, number of film-friendly casts and crew and its myriad things for filmmakers to do and see during their off hours.

The city of Las Vegas, New Mexico, also has had some good success in drawing studio people to that city, which is about an hour north of Santa Fe. One of the films known to have been made in the Meadow City was a documentary featuring boxers Jack Johnson and "Fireman" Jim Flynn in a prize bout that took place on a very hot Fourth of July in 1912. The day after the fight, the Associated Press reported:

> *Flynn displayed no ability throughout the fight. Flynn was cut about the face and by the sixth round, he was deliberately trying to butt the champion's chin with his head. Time after time, as Johnson held him powerless in the clinches, Flynn jerked his head upward. The referee warned him repeatedly, but it did no good. Flynn told the referee, "He's hold me, he's holding me!" In the seventh round, he began leaping upward every time he could work his head under Johnson's chin. The fight was stopped in the ninth round by the*

The Dog House, a real and operating restaurant, was used several times in the very popular series *Breaking Bad. Courtesy of the Wikimedia Commons.*

state police, who declared it a brutal exhibition. The referee then announced that Johnson had won and the fight was over.

Frederick Turner, writing for *Antiques the Magazine*, said:

> *The fight itself, held on Independence Day, proved a bitter event for those who had come to see the "white hope" dethrone the insolent black man who had installed his white female companion at ringside and chatted with her while brushing aside the Fireman's clumsy charges. Finally, in the ninth round, the police stopped the bout because of Flynn's flagrant fouling. Such was the town's only brush with sports history.*

Las Vegas has also hosted numerous other features over the years and has worked very hard to maintain its Hollywood connections. Films big and small have been shot in and around the city, which also boasts one of the state's last drive-in theaters, the Fort Union, which was recently saved by a fundraiser that allowed it to go digital and remain in business.

Although it has been a long time since the silent films made by Romaine Fielding and Tom Mix, Las Vegas attracted a number of productions in the '70s, including an odd little horror film starring Richard Crenna titled *The Evil*. New Mexico's only Christmas-themed film was shot in the Las Vegas area, the made-for-television movie *Miracle in the Wilderness* (1992), although crooner Perry Como came to New Mexico to do a fun Christmas special in Santa Fe and Lamy in 1979. More recently, a German crew traveled all around the state, including to Las Vegas, in 2008 to make a film that was never released in the United States, a buddy road trip movie called *Friendship*. Tommy Lee Jones was in the state a few years later to film the esoteric western *The Homesman* (2014).

Elsewhere in this book is information on the first films shot in Albuquerque, and there are newsreel clips of former president Teddy Roosevelt visiting Albuquerque that were shot in 1916. Roosevelt was in town in late October of that year to speak in support of the Republican presidential candidate, Charles Evans Hughes. Although not movies, per se, this has historical value that needs to be noted.

Santa Fe's first known film is thought to be a 1910 silent piece called *Two Lucky Jims*. This short film is said to be a western comedy about two guys—both named Jim, one fat and one skinny—the girl they are both in love with and their exploits to win the lass's heart! A copy of the movie has yet to be found.

A short documentary was shot in 1912, the year of statehood, simply entitled *Santa Fe*, but it wasn't until 1936 that another movie was made near the city, the Oscar-nominated western *The Texas Rangers*.

Things certainly blossomed from there. Besides films shot in or near the city such as *We're the Millers* (2013), *3:10 to Yuma* (2007), *Paul* (2011) and *The Silencers* (1966), the area also boasts two movie ranches, which have been used in a number of movies. It is fun to note that most movies with Santa Fe in the title were not filmed anywhere near the city, other than 1997's comedy-drama *Santa Fe*.

The Bonanza Creek Ranch was formerly known as the Jarrett Ranch. In the mid-1950s, Jimmy Stewart was in the area filming *The Man from Laramie*. Around that time, a local man, Louie Clifford, who had once been Mary Pickford's chauffeur, started a cab company in Albuquerque, fifty miles south. Clifford, who had once worked in Hollywood, maintained some Tinseltown connections and would sometimes bring Hollywood studio executives to the ranch to show them the eye-catching views. It didn't take long for some of them to see the potential in this little corner of the world. It was only a couple

Jimmy Stewart on location in northern New Mexico in *The Man from Laramie*. *Courtesy of Columbia Pictures.*

years later when a western starring Glenn Ford and Jack Lemmon was shot mostly around the ranch. *Cowboy* (1958) was the film, and it included 1,200 steers brought to New Mexico from old Mexico, thus making them co-stars in this unique western directed by Delmar Daves.

After that came the first network television series to be shot in New Mexico in 1962. *Empire* was about a modern-day cattleman/oilman and the

NEW MEXICO FILMMAKING

Bonanza Creek Movie Ranch has been used in many western films since opening in the 1980s. *Courtesy of Ken Piorkowski Photography.*

problems he faced trying to run his operations. The series starred Richard Egan, who also had a small part in a film that offered a brief glimpse of New Mexico in 1972, *Moonfire*.

Bonanza Creek has hosted numerous other productions, including *Easy Rider* (1969), *The Missing* (2003) and *Wild Hogs* (2007). Bonanza Creek has also hosted numerous television productions, including the Italian comedy western series *Lucky Luke*, which began in 1991. In 1993, two popular television series, *Gunsmoke* and *Walker, Texas Ranger*, filmed episodes at the movie ranch.

Eaves Movie Ranch began as part of a working ranch known as Rancho Allegre and was owned by J.W. Eaves. The first production to film there was the television series *Empire*, which was on location beginning in 1962. The first feature film shot there was *Where Angels Go, Trouble Follows* (1968), a fun romp starring Rosalind Russell. At one point in that movie, after the bus that Russell and her students are traveling in breaks down, she stands by the side of the road, looks both ways and mutters, "Doesn't anyone live in New Mexico?" This picture includes Robert Taylor's last film appearance.

In 1969, *The Cheyenne Social Club*, starring Jimmy Stewart and Henry Fonda, came to the area for filming. Director Gene Kelly of *Singin' in the Rain* fame

Eaves Movie Ranch, one of three western "towns" used for film shoots in New Mexico. *Courtesy of Ken Piorkowski Photography.*

"They went thataway!" On location for an unknown western shoot near Albuquerque, New Mexico, one of over two hundred westerns shot at least in part in the state. *Courtesy of John Armijo.*

worked with Eaves to create a western movie set that has since hosted more than forty film and television productions, including *Wyatt Earp* (1994), the hysterically bawdy western *Lust in the Dust* (1985) and *Silverado* (1985). Several other films were shot in and on a nearby set, which was later demolished.

About twenty-five miles south and east of Santa Fe near the village of Galisteo is the Cook Ranch, now sometimes referred to as the Cerro Pelon Ranch, after a fire started by carelessly used pyrotechnics during the filming of *Wild Wild West* (1999) burned the original set to the ground. It has hosted about twenty-five productions, including 1998's *The Hi-Lo Country* and the 1995 Japanese-made western *East Meets West*.

In southern New Mexico is the "No Name" western town between Deming and Las Cruces, but apparently, it is still waiting for its first film crew to take advantage of it.

Rancho de Los Golondrinas, a living history museum devoted to Spanish Colonial life, is also a popular spot for filmmakers, having been the host to nearly twenty titles, including *Gambler III: The Legend Continues* (1985), *Vampires* (1998) and *All the Pretty Horses* (2000).

Southern New Mexico is often left in the dust when it comes to screen productions. Bits and pieces of larger films—such as a couple of the Indiana Jones titles—have used that part of the state, but in general, any town south of Albuquerque struggles for recognition in the world of film and television.

Part of that problem might relate to the populace. In 2009, the big-budget film *Due Date*, with several big-name actors, including Robert Downey Jr., was in Las Cruces to do some second unit work. Due to poor planning, the movie crew unintentionally tied up traffic during "rush hour" (such as it is in a city of eighty thousand) for a couple of days and created such a stink among the locals that not a single production of note has come to Las Cruces to film anything since. Word gets around fast in the world of movies about who is friendly and who is not, and this odd debacle caused by the citizenry might not have done the city any favors. The city also seems incapable of hiring a film commissioner who has any actual movie experience or who wants to stay with the job.

New Mexico has done what might be called "stand in" work for many places over the years. It has been used as Texas countless times in films such as *The Texas Rangers* (1936), *El Paso* (1949), *Streets of Laredo* (1949), *The Ballad of Gregorio Cortez* (1982), *Astronaut Farmer* (2006) and *The Dry Land* (2010). It has been Russia in *Skyjacked* (1972), nameless places in South America in *Sorcerer* (1977) and Nebraska in the telemovie *Peter Lundy and the Medicine Hat Stallion* (1977). The state has also played Africa numerous times in movies

Blind Horizon, a 1993 release, relied on viewers to once again accept amnesia as common—and that New Mexico is Texas. New Mexico has "starred" as Texas in dozens of movies and television shows. *Courtesy of John Armijo.*

like *The Light that Failed* (1939), *Sundown* (1941), *The Desert Song* (1943), *Sudan* (1945), *Night without Stars* (1949) and *King Solomon's Mines* (1950). These films used areas on the Navajo (Dine) Nation, Gallup's Red Rock State Park and Carlsbad Caverns and vicinity for the Sahara Desert or the Espanola area north of Santa Fe.

Charlize Theron in *North Country*, based on the true story of a woman's fight to work in the mines. *Courtesy of the Warner Brothers Studio.*

Red Dawn (1984) was shot mostly around Las Vegas, which portrayed Colorado; *North Country* (2005) saw the Silver City area filling in for Minnesota. Some of the state landscape has also appeared as Mars (*John Carpenter's Ghosts of Mars*, 2000) and as a twin planet of Earth in the NBC television series *Earth 2*, which was on air in 1994–95 and is often credited with reviving the film industry in New Mexico—but one would tend to think those who say so hadn't done much research about the past work made in state. Carlsbad Caverns also "stars" as the center of Earth in the 1951 opus *Unknown World*.

The 1994 release of *Wyatt Earp* saw the state being used as Texas, Kansas and Arizona. In *Fan Boys* (2008), the filmmakers really should have consulted a road map since they use New Mexico as a location for Iowa, Ohio, Nevada and California, certainly using very careful editing to ensure that a prickly pear cactus didn't appear in the scenes set in Iowa.

The record for number of places that New Mexico appears in one work as someplace else probably has to go to the USA Network television series *In Plain Sight*, which ran for five seasons from 2008 to 2012. In depicting an Albuquerque-based U.S. marshal, played by Mary McCormack, the directors and crew were able to have the Land of Enchantment appear as

Indiana; Tennessee; Denver, Colorado; Philadelphia, Pennsylvania; New Jersey; Chicago, Illinois; and Los Angeles, California.

Traveling out of Earth's bounds, science fiction has also been a popular subject in the fervent imaginations of filmmakers—*The Man Who Fell to Earth* (1976), *Contact* (1997), *2010: The Year We Make Contact* (1985) and *Tank Girl* (1995) used White Sands National Monument for a few scenes. At one point during the shooting of *Tank Girl*, a record temperature of 126 degrees Fahrenheit was recorded while filming in the summer of 1994. *Armageddon* (1998) and *Independence Day* (1996) both concern threats from outer space—a meteor and aliens, respectively—and the aliens return in *Independence Day: Resurgence* (2016) when they resurface to create more havoc and mischief on our fair planet.

Much of the New Mexico content for *Independence Day* actually ended up on the floor of the editing room, and *Contact* (1997) only briefly used the Very Large Array (VLA) Telescope near Socorro to advance its story, which starred Jodie Foster. The VLA consists of twenty-seven huge dish antennas situated on the San Agustin Plains, west of Socorro, New Mexico. Each is nearly one hundred feet tall and eighty-two feet in diameter and placed in a Y-shaped configuration, allowing astronomers to "study radio waves emitted by distant objects," including planets, stars and even other galaxies.

Another sci-fi film that is often credited to New Mexico is the still-scary 1954 release *Them*, which is about atomic energy–infused giant ants. The film is set in New Mexico but was actually made in California. The desert scenes clearly show Joshua trees, which do not grow in New Mexico.

Oddly, in spite of the state's fame via supposed UFO crashes and sightings, most especially in an area north of Roswell, no real feature films have been done to offer a believer's-eye view of this incident. There have been many documentaries, both amateur and professional, about this 1947 case, but even though a couple features have been made that use the "crash" loosely, none has been shot in New Mexico, including the 1999 television series *Roswell* that ran for three seasons and never left California or the 1994 made-for-television movie of the same name that was completed in southern Arizona.

And here is a spoiler for those who may believe a UFO did crash thirty miles north of Roswell in 1947: if you carefully read the story and related articles, it takes about three minutes to rebuff the whole thing, although it has helped turn Roswell into a tourist mecca.

More recently, perhaps lured by the state's tax incentives for filmmakers as well as geography, New Mexico has taken turns as Afghanistan in *Lone Survivor* (2014) and *Seal Team Six: The Raid on Osama Bin Laden*. In *The Boys of Abu Ghraib* (2011), New Mexico briefly portrayed Iraq. *The Men Who Stare at Goats* (2009) also used New Mexico locales for some of its Middle East settings.

We won't even try to count the number of times that New Mexico has appeared as old Mexico. Other films have also made New Mexico appear as Munich, Germany; Israel; Cincinnati; and Memphis (*Elvis Has Left the Building*, 2004). None of the King's thirty-one movies ever used New Mexico as a shooting location, but over the years, he did appear twice in Albuquerque, once in April 1956 when he performed at the Armory. Tickets cost $1.50 and 5,000 screaming fans attended. Elvis Presley returned in April 1972, playing to 11,857 adoring people at the Tingley Coliseum. Curiously, fifteen of the twenty songs he performed were covers. Presley might have snuck into town on occasion as well, at least according to this quote from the City of Albuquerque website. Emma Moya wrote, "Elvis Presley would come in from California through Gallup in his pink Cadillac and watch the lights of Albuquerque from the top of Nine Mile Hill. Everybody knew when he was coming, and we would watch him at the filling station."

CASTS AND CREWS

During the course of the research for this book, it became glaringly obvious that even though New Mexico has an incredible moviemaking history, there are some important omissions concerning women and people of color.

Few films that have been shot in the state have featured people from the African American and Hispanic communities, they have often shown American Indians in a negative light and there have been few strong roles for women and only a handful of opportunities for female directors.

Examples of this are numerous, and what is sometimes even more embarrassing is the fact that often when a lead role for a person of color was available, it was given to an Anglo who was then given "red face" or "brown face."

Redskin, the state's last silent film, did make an attempt to portray Native people in a positive light, but it used Anglo actor Richard Dix as its star. Dix also did another "red face" movie, *The Vanishing American*.

In the aforementioned films where New Mexico portrays Africa, not one legitimate African person appears in them, even substituting character actor Andy Devine for an Egyptian.

The 1942 comedy-western *Valley of the Sun* portrays First Nations people as goofy buffoons who all dress in Plains Indian garb, while 1970's *Flap* does the same thing in a somewhat different way—while claiming to hold the tribal people in high regard, it uses actors like Anthony Quinn and Claude Akins, both non–American Indians, both alcohol infused, in lead roles.

Although it is a great movie that brought an Academy Award nomination to an actor who had some Spanish lineage, Thomas Gomez, the makers of *Ride the Pink Horse* (1947) also cast "wholesome, green-eyed" Wanda Hendrix as Pila, a young Mexican woman who falls for and assists Lucky Gagen in his pursuit of the man who wronged him. Jerry Lewis does a humiliating turn as a Native American in *My Friend Irma Goes West* (1950), and the famous 1971 release *Billy Jack* makes a less awkward mistake by having star and director Tom Laughlin portray a person of mixed heritage, including American Indian.

The first film to really offer a good role for a Latino was the documentary version of *...And Now Miguel* (1953), which featured the "real" Miguel as a young boy who wants to become a shepherd.

The picture has an interesting history, starting with accidental filmmaker Joseph Krumgold, who began his career as a screenwriter in Hollywood and made *...And Now Miguel* as a film for the United States government.

Krumgold and his wife lived with the Chavez family in Los Cordovas, near Taos in northern New Mexico, for several months throughout the filming of *...And Now Miguel.*

The film was so well received that the Thomas Y. Crowell publishing company asked him to write a children's book based on the film. The book, published in 1953, won Krumgold the prestigious Newbery Medal for Excellence in American Children's Literature. Krumgold continued his career as an author and became the first person to ever win the Newbery Medal twice. The second time was in 1960 for his book *Onion John.*

After *...And Now Miguel* was completed, Krumgold encouraged young Miguel Chavez to move to New York and take acting lessons. However, Chavez's father did not allow it.

"I've lived the way I wanted to live," said Chavez in a 2008 interview with Turner Classic Movies as he looked back at the force the film had on his life. "And I wouldn't change my life...for millions and millions of dollars."

Chavez operated a handcrafted furniture business for thirty years before retiring. He also married, raised a family and became a highly skilled woodcarver. He noted in that interview, "Even today when I walk into a grocery store," said Chavez, "someone yells out, 'Hey, it's now Miguel!' I swear one of these days I'm going to die and they're going to write on my tombstone, 'And Now Miguel Passed Away'…Because of the film and the book, I still get letters and calls from people all over the world."

In 1966, a feature film of the same name was released, starring an Anglo lad, Pat Cardi, as Miguel and Michael Ansara as his father, an actor who was born in Syria.

A fun aside for this film is that Ray Burwick—a noted bird trainer and wrangler who also worked on the Hitchcock film *The Birds* and the Burt Lancaster vehicle *The Birdman of Alcatraz*—was working on a scene where one of his trained eagles was to attack one of Miguel's lambs, but instead it flew away, never to be seen again. Thankfully for the production, that eagle had a stand-in that did the job.

The one film that did break many of these stereotypes and cast non-Anglo actors was *Salt of the Earth* (1954), which used real Latino and Latina untrained actors and actresses and gave many strong roles to women.

Sea of Grass offered a sturdy role to Katharine Hepburn, opposite Spencer Tracy. She plays Lutie, the lonely wife of Tracy's character, Jim, whose huge cattle ranch demands his constant attention. Adultery and drama ensue, but Hepburn carries her character well for the time the movie was shot, 1947.

In *Make Haste to Live*, a 1954 release shot partially in the Taos area, actress Dorothy McGuire played a good characterization of a successful woman fleeing a bad marriage. Rosalind Russell, among others, starred in the first film with a mostly female cast, *Where Angels Go, Trouble Follows*, released in 1968.

The '70s brought a spate of roles for African Americans, although most of the films were low-budget western, while the 1971 television series *The City* (aka *Man in the City*) had native Mexican actor Anthony Quinn starring as the mayor of a big city in the southwestern United States, not unlike Albuquerque, where it was shot.

Gene Layman, an African American actor, had a co-starring role in *White Renegade*, the first sound film shot in New Mexico, back in 1931, but it really wasn't until 1996 when Will Smith landed a role in *Independence Day* that a black actor took a major role in a New Mexico–made film. Black actresses still await their chance at this writing.

Women in general have received a few plum roles. Sometimes they get them in outstanding small-budget films such as Karen Young in *Warrior Woman* (2011) and Joan Allen in *Georgia O'Keeffe* (2009), both of which are excellent movies. In terms of bigger films with good roles for women, *The Homesman* (2014) starred Hilary Swank and *We're the Millers* (2013) featured Jennifer Aniston.

Things have changed a bit for the Hispanic acting community in recent years, especially with the release of the outstanding *Bless Me Ultima* (2013), which not only starred Latino and Latina actors but was also directed by an African American, Carl Franklin.

The 1988 release of the *The Milagro Beanfield War* was hailed as a breakthrough for the Hispanic community, although there was some grumbling about the lack of ethnic purity, even though director Robert Redford employed a number of Hispanic department heads, including the production designer, production manager and construction coordinator. *Becoming Eduardo*, a strong 2008 release directed by Rod McCall that had much success at film festivals, featured a break for Hispanic actor Julian Alcaraz.

American Indian cast members received a few minor breaks along the way, but not many. The 1964 western *A Distant Trumpet* does use some tribal people (uncredited) in the cast instead of Anglos in red face, and there is a very interesting and funny clip on the documentary film *Reel Injun* that translates accurately what one of the those actors is actually saying in the Dine language to cavalry officer Troy Donohue during a meeting between the cavalry and warriors. The translation allows that the scolding Donohue, according to the Dine warrior, is a "snake rolling in his own shit," which I don't think was actually in the script!

Other strong roles for Native American actors in recent years include a couple based on Tony Hillerman books, *A Thief of Time* (2004) and *Coyote Waits* (2003). Noted American Indian Chris Eyre (*Smoke Signals*) directed these two great films. Both films featured American Indian actors Wes Studi and Gary Farmer (both residents of Santa Fe), Adam Beach, Sheila Tousey and Graham Greene.

An excellent miniseries made for the Turner Network and on air in 2005 was called *Into the West*. Part of this series was filmed in New Mexico and had a number of recurring roles that featured Native actors, including Tousey, Eric Schweig, Irene Bedard, Joseph Marshall III and the late Russell Means. Means also co-starred in *Tiger Eyes* (2013), one of his last film roles, which also featured his son, Tatanka Means, in a starring role. The 2014 release of the micro-budget *Drunktown's Finest* uses almost all new Native actors for the lead roles.

A few women have had the chance to direct movie shoots in New Mexico, among them Rachel Talalay for *Tank Girl* and Mirra Bank for the PBS documentary *Nobody's Girls: Five Women of the West*, with both of these productions being released in 1995. Antonia Bird directed *Mad Love* (1995), which has a few New Mexico scenes, as did *Committed*, from 2000, directed by Lisa Krueger.

Alexandra Pratt was director, co-producer and co-writer of the 1997 film *The Trailblazer*, which was never released. This $300,000-budget film offers a look at a wilderness program designed to help troubled young people.

Karen Bartlett directed the PBS documentary *Mary Jane Colter: House Made of Dawn* in 1997 as well.

Julie Riechert's *Warrior Woman* had a small 2012 release; Vanessa Vassar's documentary, *Cinderellas of Santa Fe*, had some screenings in 2006; and Michele Ohayon had some success with her terrific 2005 documentary, *Cowboy del Amour*.

The *Tao of Steve* was directed by Jenniphr Goodman and released in 2000, and hopefully other work from her is coming soon. Niki Caro was in New Mexico in 2004 to direct *North Country*; Anne Feinsilber came to New Mexico to work on her unique documentary *Requiem for Billy the Kid*, which was released in 2007; and Christine Jeffs of New Zealand used New Mexico to film the 2009 release *Sunshine Cleaning*.

Patricia Riggen directed the 2011 Disney Channel picture *Lemonade Mouth*. More recently, the superb *Drunktown's Finest* was directed by Sydney Freeland, who is a member of the Dine Nation and was born and raised near Gallup, New Mexico, where the film takes place. Freeland is also probably the first transgender person to direct a film in New Mexico.

The door opener seems to be Allison Anders, who was a real pioneer, filming her 1992 release *Gas, Food, Lodging* in the far southwestern New Mexico town of Deming, a place she later said she picked for its desolation.

Mimi Leder did a made-for-television piece the next year, *Rio Shannon*, which was a failed pilot for a television show about a woman restoring a ranch, which screened on the ABC network.

Besides Franklin's directing of *Bless Me Ultima*, it might be true that there are only two other New Mexico–made movies directed by an African American. One was the oddball flick *Don't Play Us Cheap*, which was seen on screens briefly in 1973 and based on director Melvin Van Pebbles's own Broadway musical. The other was the western *Adios, Amigo* (1976), which was done by Fred Williamson, who also stars. With tongue firmly in cheek, comedian Richard Pryor co-stars as a character named Sam Spade.

The gay, lesbian, bisexual and transgender community has also not received a lot of attention in New Mexico. Only a few pictures have GLBT characters, including the ultra silly and fun *Horror in the Wind* (2008), the documentary feature *The Truth or Consequences of Delmar Howe* (2004) and a very small part of *Brokeback Mountain* (2005). In particular, the GLBT field is wide open since one of the biggest GLBT film festivals in the country, the Southwest Gay and Lesbian Film Festival, occurs in Albuquerque each autumn.

There might be others that I have overlooked, but nonetheless there is a great imbalance in all of this, one that will hopefully right itself as more and more film and TV productions come to New Mexico.

9

READ THE BOOK, SEE THE MOVIE

A number of films with a New Mexico connection also have connections to literary works.

The last silent film shot in New Mexico, *Redskin*, was based on a novel called *Navajo* by Elizabeth Pickett.

Rudyard Kipling's 1890 novel *The Light that Failed* was the basis for the film of the same title.

John Steinbeck's famous *Grapes of Wrath* became the first—and, to date, the only—movie that utilizes the world-famous Route 66 by using some second unit shots in New Mexico.

Thanks God, I'll Take It from Here became a John Wayne vehicle that spent a little time in Raton, New Mexico. The film version was called *Without Reservations*, and the book was written by Jane Allen and Mae Livingston. The movie was made before the book was released!

The 1947 release *Sea of Grass* was based on a work by Conrad Richter.

Ride the Pink Horse was a novel by Dorothy B. Hughes.

Frederic Wakeman wrote the book *The Hucksters*, which was made into a movie starring Clark Gable and has a few brief New Mexico scenes.

Four Faces West was made from Eugene Manlove Rhodes's novelette *Pasó por Aquí*.

H. Rider Haggard's work *King Solomon's Mines* has been on screen five times since the first production in 1919. The 1950 version was partially shot in New Mexico.

Night without Stars is a film based on the novel by Winston Graham, with a bit of second unit work done in southern New Mexico.

The 1951 release *Only the Valiant* was filmed mostly around Gallup and was based on a novel by Charles Marquis Warren.

George and Helen Papishvivy wrote the novel *Anything Can Happen*, which became a film released in 1952. This picture was also shot partially around the town of Gallup.

...And Now Miguel, one of the more famous pieces of New Mexico–connected literature, was done by Joseph Krumgold. It was both a feature film and a documentary, with Krumgold winning the Newbery Award for the book.

Another novelist, Mildred Gordon, saw her book *Make Haste to Live* come to the big screen in 1954, with that movie shot partially around Taos.

Frank Harris's memoir about his days as a cowboy came to the silver screen in *Cowboy*, a film that starred Jack Lemmon and Glen Ford.

Although not a book, *Left Handed Gun* was based on a play written by Gore Vidal and was made into a movie twice, with the 1958 version having a few scenes shot in New Mexico.

Journey to the Center of the Earth is based on the famed novel by Jules Verne.

Edward Abbey saw his masterpiece *The Last Cowboy* come to the big screen as *Lonely Are the Brave*.

A one-time resident of New Mexico, Paul Horgan wrote *A Distant Trumpet*, which was partially shot in northwestern New Mexico.

Although it wasn't based on a book, per se, the television pilot, *Calhoun: County Agent* did find itself connected to literature when Merle Miller, who wrote the teleplay, later wrote a sardonic and name-dropping book about his experiences in trying to get the series made. The title is *Only You, Dick Daring!; or, How to Write One Television Script and Make $50,000,000.*

The year 1965 was the release date for the comedy western *The Hallelujah Trail*, based on a work by Bill Gulick.

The 1970 film *Up in the Cellar* was based on a book by Angus Hall.

Clair Huffaker's novel *Nobody Loves a Drunken Indian* became the basis for the 1970 movie *Flap*.

One of New Mexico's best movies is *Red Sky at Morning*, based on a novel by Richard Bradford, who lived in Santa Fe for some time.

Richard Widmark starred in *When the Legends Die*, which was based on a novel by Hal Borland. It was shot in part in northwest New Mexico.

The only western that John Wayne made in the state, *The Cowboys*, used a book by William Dale Jennings as its source material. It is curious to think that Wayne did this film since Jennings was an early advocate

Calhoun: County Agent, New Mexico's favorite failed TV pilot, shot in Las Cruces and Mesilla, New Mexico. *Courtesy of* Las Cruces Bulletin *and David Salcido.*

of gay rights and a founder of the Mattachine Society, one of the first groups to support same.

Jim Kane was the name of the novel that J.P.S. Brown wrote that became the movie entitled *Pocket Money*.

Jonathan Livingston Seagull, by Richard Bach, became a movie of the same name, which had a few scenes shot in Carlsbad Caverns.

Based on a book by Walter Tevis, *The Man Who Fell to Earth* brought David Bowie to New Mexico to make the movie.

The slightly cryptic western *The White Buffalo* was based on a book by Richard Sale.

A made-for-television movie, *Peter Lundy and the Medicine Hat Stallion*, was filmed in New Mexico and based on a novel by Marguerite Henry.

Author Marilyn Harris's work *Hatter Fox* became the made-for-TV film *Lost Legacy: A Girl Called Hatter Fox*.

John McPhee wrote a short story, "Ruidoso," which later became the fun Walter Matthau movie *Casey's Shadow*. McPhee later won a Pulitzer Prize for his nonfiction work *Annals of the Former World*.

A Shining Season was made into a made-for-TV movie and screened in 1979. It was based on a book by William Buchanan.

Leslie Waller is the same author who wrote the book that the hit movie *Dog Day Afternoon* was based on. She also wrote the book that the New Mexico made movie *Hide in Plain Sight* was adapted from.

Dan Greenburg is responsible for the novel that the bawdy film *Private Lessons* is based on.

Wrong Is Right, from 1982, is based on the book *The Better Angels* by writer Charles McCarry.

Arthur C. Clarke (*2001: A Space Odyssey*) also wrote the novel *2010*, which was later made into the film *2010: The Year We Make Contact*, part of which was shot in central New Mexico.

Lucian Truscott IV wrote a novel that became *Dress Gray*, a 1985 teleplay that was filmed at the New Mexico Military Institute in Roswell, New Mexico.

Certainly one of the most revered films that has been made in New Mexico is *The Milagro Beanfield War*, which was the first of a trilogy written by Taos-based author John Nichols.

Tabor Evans is a pseudonym for a number of authors who wrote a series of western novels about a character named Longarm, which was made into a television movie that screened in 1988.

Stretching things just a bit, *Cultivating Charlie*, a 1988 release, is loosely based on Voltaire's *Candide*.

The famous television miniseries, *Lonesome Dove* was based on works by Larry McMurtry, who earlier had won a Pulitzer Prize for the book. McMurtry leads the league in New Mexico–based productions, as his work has also been screened for a couple of other television miniseries, including *Buffalo Girls*, *Comanche Moon* and the screenplay for *Brokeback Mountain*, which came from a short story by Annie Proulx.

The 1991 television production *Miracle in the Wilderness* is from a novel written by Paul Gallico. Gallico also wrote the novel *The Poseidon Adventure*, which became the huge hit film of the same name, released in 1972.

Gas, Food, Lodging, a 1992 release, was from a novel by Richard Peck.

Alan Martin and Jamie Hewlett are the creators of the comic strip that *Tank Girl* was based on.

Spike Lee adapted Richard Price's book *Clockers* for the big screen. A very small part of the film was shot in New Mexico.

Richard Feynman, an author and physicist, saw his books *Surely You're Joking, Mr. Feynman!* and *What Do You Care What Other People Think?* made into the film *Infinity*, released in 1996.

Famed writer Elmore Leonard had has book *Last Stand at Saber River* turned into a television movie. His short story later became the hit feature *3:10 to Yuma*. Another work based on characters he created was made into the television film *Desperado: Avalanche at Devil's Ridge*.

Another big name in literature, Carl Sagan, wrote the novel *Contact*, which became the 1997 film starring Jodie Foster. A small part of this flicker was shot in central New Mexico.

Certainly one of the best books ever written about life as a real cowboy, *The Hi-Lo Country* by Max Evans, became a movie in 1998, directed by Englishman Stephen Frears, who was quoted at the Santa Fe Film Festival as saying, "I always wanted to direct a western, and now I have!"

Still another famed author, Vladimir Nobokov, has a small New Mexico connection. The 1997 remake of *Lolita* had a small part of the film shot here.

Cormac McCarthy, who lives in the Santa Fe area, was the author of *All the Pretty Horses*, which was put onto the big screen in 2000. The book won the National Book Award in 1992. Another of McCarthy's works was the luminous New Mexico–made *No Country for Old Men*, which won four Oscars, including one for Best Picture in 2007.

McCarthy also wrote a play, *The Sunset Unlimited*, with the film version being shot in New Mexico.

Two books came out after the chilling documentary *The Silence of Cricket Coogler* was released in 2000. *Cricket in the Web* by Paula Moore, a thoroughly researched book about one of New Mexico's grittiest and unsolved crimes, was followed in 2005 by *Murder Near the Crosses* by Peter Sandman, the son of one of the state police officers who worked on the case.

A film directed by Ron Howard and released in 2003, *The Missing*, came from the novel by Thomas Eidson.

Tony Hillerman is probably one of New Mexico's best-known and most popular writers. Several of his books were turned into films that were shot in New Mexico including *A Dark Wind*, *Coyote Waits* and *A Thief of Time*, with the latter two works being made for PBS Television.

North Country was based on a popular tome entitled *Class Action: The Story of Lois Jensen and the Landmark Case that Changed Sexual Harassment Law* by Clara Bingham and Laura Leedy.

Some second unit shooting was done in New Mexico for the film version of *Rent*, which was written by Jonathan Larson, who tragically died at age thirty-five.

Marsha Recknagle saw her novel *If Nights Could Talk* come to the small screen with a new title, *In from the Night*.

The winner of the best title for a book/movie is *The Men Who Stare at Goats*, written by Jon Ronson, who also did the screenplay for the 2014 film *Frank*, a small portion of which was shot in New Mexico.

Author Jim Thompson—who was blacklisted during the McCarthy communist hunt in the '50s and later became an alcoholic and died when he starved himself to death—wrote the work that *The Killer Inside Me* is based on.

The wonderful 2010 remake of *True Grit* came from the pen of author Charles Portis.

Tiger Eyes, by bestselling author Judy Blume, was shot in New Mexico and released in 2013. Blume's books have sold over seventy-five million copies worldwide.

Peter Fromm is the author of *As Cool as I Am*, which was made into a film released in 2013.

One of the finest New Mexico–based books was turned into one of the finest New Mexico–made movies when Rudolfo Anaya's coming-of-age tale, *Bless Me Ultima*, was released at last in 2013.

Another bestselling writer, Dean R. Koontz, saw his mystery-fantasy *Odd Thomas* come to the screen in 2013. The film was shot mostly in Santa Fe and Albuquerque.

Longmire, a hugely successful cable series, was dropped by its originator because it wanted a younger audience but is now part of Netflix. New Mexico "stars" as Wyoming. *Courtesy of A&E.*

A gentleman named Sidney Carroll wrote the short story that both versions of *Gambit* were based on, with a small part of the 2013 remake being shot in New Mexico.

Goats, a 2013 release as well, was from a novel by Mark Poirier.

Marcus Luttrell, a combat veteran, wrote the true story about his experiences in war for *Lone Survivor*.

Craig Johnson wrote the series of mystery/crime novels that the hugely popular cable TV series *Longmire* is based on.

I'm sure there are some that I have missed and that there will be many more to come in the future as well. I didn't really touch on the comic books and graphic novels that have found a home in New Mexico (*Thor*, *Ironman*, *Superman*), but this will give you a good idea of the literary hooks that New Mexico has had. Who knows, maybe someday, someone will find a way to turn this fine book into a movie!

10

SHOW ME THE (TAX) MONEY

Breaking Bad ended up in Albuquerque because of the [state tax] incentives. It was originally conceived to film in California, but Sony Pictures Television wanted to take advantage of the [New Mexico] film incentives. Vince Gilligan [the creator of the series] came to visit Albuquerque, and fell in love with it!" says Albuquerque Film Liaison Ann Lerner. Lerner has been in the position for over ten years and has certainly seen a lot of results of the financial incentives offered to filmmakers.

Breaking Bad certainly was at the forefront of the new wave of shows and movies that have been made at least in part in New Mexico. The series, which has a record number of viewers and was nominated for nearly two hundred awards, has become part of New Mexico culture. Who'd have thought that a high school teacher with cancer and a slacker with connections could provide so much interest that many people admit to binging on episode after episode of the well-written and well-acted series. As a bonus, it really takes place in New Mexico, rather than having New Mexico play-act as Los Angeles or somewhere less exotic than the state that sits between Arizona and Texas that many people don't know about.

Since the advent of the incentive program in 2002, over three hundred productions have found at least a temporary home in the state. And some of that money that that has brought in has been spread around the state, with even some smaller communities seeing film productions come to town. *The Rambler* (2013) was filmed partially in tiny Dexter, near Roswell, and Sunland Park, a town on the Mexican border, hosted *50 to 1* (2014) and *Death Valley* (2004).

Fans of the enormously popular television series *Breaking Bad* helped increase the business at the Octopus Car Wash, which was recently sold and renamed. *Courtesy of John Armijo.*

The program currently offers 25 percent in rebates to film companies for most expenses that occur in state. Any production wishing to qualify for the program must shoot at least 80 percent of its work in New Mexico in order to qualify. Additional legislation has been added since the program began in 2002 under then governor Gary Johnson.

Bill Richardson followed Johnson as governor and was very supportive of the program, raising the credit to 25 percent from 15 percent.

Supplementary benefits began in 2013 when "long running television programs" became eligible for an additional 5 percent incentive. The production companies must file a state tax return to receive the credit, and then they receive a direct deposit or check to cover the cost.

Loans are also available to studios, offering market interest rates, although this program has not been used very often.

Governor Suzanne Martinez, who followed Richardson into office, wanted to either roll back the program or eliminate it entirely, something she tried to do in 2011, until she finally saw the big picture and reduced the cutbacks that had been passed. Martinez was able to cap the incentive payouts at $50 million, which slowed the industry considerably.

When reading why Governor Martinez was doing so, it became apparent that she just saw the program as a way for opportunistic studios to take advantage of the state while not grasping the idea of how much money was brought into the state for local businesses since the crews and cast members would be spending plenty of money on food, lodging, equipment, salaries and transportation.

Between 2010 and 2014, $251 million in tax incentives were paid out, which helped create 117 jobs for every $1 million spent.

New Mexico's film industry has pumped $1.5 billion into the state's economy during those years, and it also helped garner $0.43 in tax revenue for every incentive dollar that was spent by the state during that same time frame. An estimated 15,848 full-time jobs have been created by film and television production companies.

Several other states mimicked New Mexico's policy for a while, and it seems that some, such as Louisiana and Georgia, have been successful in luring movie crews to their states. Others—such as Arizona, Indiana, Kansas and Iowa—do not have incentive programs. In 2015, thirty-nine states had incentive programs for movie and television production.

The highlights of the New Mexico program are as follows:

- A 25 percent refundable credit applies to resident cast and crew and in-state rentals, purchases and services from New Mexico vendors.
- A 5 percent additional credit for qualified TV series.
- A 5 percent additional credit on below-the-line resident crew compensation if filming a certain number of days at a qualified production facility.
- Productions may be able to qualify certain nonresident below-the-line positions if they cannot find local hires and certain contributions are made to workforce development efforts.
- Payments for nonresident performing artists can qualify if paid via a "super loan-out" company subject to various New Mexico taxes.
- There is a $5 million credit cap for all performing artists.
- There is no minimum spending amount; $50 million is the rolling cap, subject to time of request for refund per year.
- Stand-alone post-production can qualify.
- The program excludes nonresident crew and non-performing artists but includes their per diem and housing.
- Credits over $2 million and less than $5 million must be taken over two years; credits over $5 million must be taken over three years, subject to annual rolling cap availability.

Where do I sign?

THE BEST MOVIES MADE IN NEW MEXICO

Personal Opinion

Ace in the Hole (1951)
All the Pretty Horses (2000)
The Ballad of Gregorio Cortez (1982)
Bless Me, Ultima (2013)
The Burning Plain (2008)
Elvis Has Left the Building (2004)
The Hi-Lo Country (1998)
The Hired Hand (1971)
Lonely Are the Brave (1962)
Lust in the Dust (1985)
The Milagro Beanfield War (1988)
No Country for Old Men (2007)
Powwow Highway (1989)
Red Sky at Morning (1971)
Ride the Pink Horse (1947)
Rocky Mountain (1950)
Salt of the Earth (1954)
Sorcerer (1977)
True Grit (2010)
Two-Lane Blacktop (1971)
White Sands (1992)
Young Guns II (1990)

BIBLIOGRAPHY

Albuquerque (NM) Journal. "Frame by Frame." January 2015.

American Film Institute Database. www.afi.com.

Armijo, John. Interviews with the author, 2011 to March 2014.

Boggs, Johnny D. *Billy the Kid on Film, 1911–2012.* Jefferson, NC: McFarland and Company, 2013.

Cargo, David Francis. *Lonesome Dave: The Story of New Mexico Governor David Francis Cargo.* Santa Fe, NM: Sunstone Press, 2010.

Cox, Dan. "Pic Print Stolen in Hollywood." *Variety* (February 17, 1994).

Evans, Max. Interviews with the author.

Frears, Stephen. Interview with the author.

Gaberscelk, Carlo, and Kenny Stier. *A Century of Western Movie Locations.* Rialto, CA: Corriganville Press, 2011.

———. *In Search of Western Movie Sets.* Rialto, CA: Jerry Schneider Enterprises, LLC, 2014.

Internet Movie Database. www.imdb.com.

Kasindorf, Martin. "Hollywood on the Rio Grande." *Pittsburgh (PA) Press,* December 27, 1970.

Las Vegas, NM, Film Tour Guide. Las Vegas, NM: Las Vegas Film Commission, 2012.

Magers, Boyd. Western Clippings. www.westernclippings.com.

Meléndez, A. Gabriel. *Hidden Chicano Cinema.* New Brunswick, NJ: Rutgers University Press, 2013.

BIBLIOGRAPHY

Melzer, Richard. *New Mexico: A Celebration of the Land of Enchantment.* Layton, UT: Gibbs Smith, 2011.

Movie Diva. www.moviediva.com.

Moving Picture World (www.archives.org), 1912–16.

New Mexico Film Office, Santa Fe, NM.

New Mexico Magazine (July–August 1973 and November 2008).

New Mexico Magazine (1998). "100 Hundred Years of Filmmaking in New Mexico."

New Mexico Office of Public Records, Santa Fe, NM.

Nott, Robert. "Lonesome Roads: Author Max Evans on the 'Hi Lo Country.'" *Santa Fe New Mexican,* May 17, 2013.

Poling, Charles C. "Movie Magic." *Santa Fean Magazine* (March 2014).

Sklowar, Max. Interview with the author.

State of New Mexico Historical Film Collection. Pamphlet, 1974.

Turner Classic Movies Database. www.tcm.com.

INDEX

INDEX

INDEX

ABOUT THE AUTHOR

Jeff Berg is a freelance writer, journalist and New Mexico film historian living in Santa Fe. He has traveled around New Mexico presenting his noted *Made in New Mexico* film clip series, doing live narration for each show. Previously, he served on the board of the Mesilla Valley Film Society, located in Mesilla, New Mexico, and was the assistant manager at the Jean Cocteau Cinema in Santa Fe.